Fore!
Good luck!
Tod M

D0939570

(To Leonard -
Have some fun
out there!)

Mulligan's Name
Was Ambrose

By Tod McGinley

Published By The Mary And Martha House, Inc.
Ruskin, Florida

MULLIGAN'S NAME WAS AMBROSE

Printed by M&M Printing Co. Inc., Ruskin, Florida 33570

International Standard Book Number
ISBN O-9664987-0-4

ILLUSTRATIONS BY HOWARD BARRY AND JACK EGAN

To Carolee,

my loving wife and mother of three great boys: Joe, Dan and Steve.

•••

Carolee is quite a golf story herself. At the Fairview Hospital in Minneapolis in 1985 she had three- and four-hour operations on two successive Fridays in January to repair spine damage from scoliosis.

Thanks to an outstanding surgeon, Dr. Robert Winter, and his crack team of assistants and nurses and the insertion of two 19" Harrington steel rods into her back, favorable results were obtained.

After a month in the hospital, Carolee was released to return to our home in Sudbury, Massachusetts. Dr. Winter predicted two things at that time. He said that she might set off some airport metal detectors (she has), and that she could not swing a golf club. But down here in warm, sunny Florida, far from the cold of Minnesota and the raw New England weather, we are happy to report that Carolee these days plays golf three times a week!

A New Publishing Trend

Since there are more than one, the dedications and acknowledgments are at the close of this book.

—CONTENTS—

A Foreword: Fiction And Non-Fiction

In America in 1998 the print media and TV often create the news as well as report it. So today's reader is probably conditioned to the "intermingling" of truth and fiction, such as Truman Capote toyed with in his work "In Cold Blood."

We surely have taken some poetic license in the story of Mulligan, although some of it is quite true, as two of my friends named Murray and Thompson might attest. Of course, the St. Anthony tale is pure fiction, and a tip off for the unsuspecting reader might be the mention of car keys. There were not any automobiles in Italy in his time, so he could not find keys to a car, let alone a gondola. We have not sought the imprimatur of any church officials for this book, although the few priests that have read it seemed to enjoy it as the clergy are usually familiar with golf courses.

So dear reader, relax, sit back and enjoy. If you are like me you can't hit a fast ball anymore, kick a football 50 yards, or put the puck in the upper right corner, but occasionally we experience that thing of beauty, a perfect golf shot, a joy forever and one just as good as any Jack, Arnie or Nancy ever hit. That's golf, friends!

(Editor's note: By his own account, McGinley has lost balls, been out of bounds and in the woods in 27 states, two Canadian provinces and the islands of Puerto Rico and St. Thomas. He has been off the course and in other places where "the sun don't shine" so often that it's amazing to us that his current medical records include a Dr. Mike Caruso, dermatologist, surgeon and golfer among his physicians.)

A Word About The
Mary And Martha House

We were very fortunate that we worked for 35 years for a firm, H.B. Fuller Co. of St. Paul, Minnesota, that stressed volunteerism and community involvement among its employees.

So when we found out that the Mary and Martha House in Hillsborough County, Florida, was a refuge for abused women and their children, we knew then what it was all about.

Most of us would agree with Mark Twain's observation that "I have been through some terrible things in my life, some of which actually happened." You can bet that the often terrified, and in transit, young women and children that seek protection at the Mary and Martha House have been through some terrible times that, indeed, have happened.

In the movie "Oh, God," John Denver, playing a supermarket manager, asks George Burns, who played God, why oh why, he didn't concentrate more on helping the people down here on earth. To which Burns (God) replied, "Listen kid, I don't sweat the small stuff... and besides, that's why I gave you each other!"

And that's what the volunteers at the Mary and Martha House, under Executive Director Priscilla Mixon and her assistant, Sr. Margaret, are dedicated to — helping others and teaching them to help themselves. God and George Burns would be pleased!

Chapter 1

Mulligan's Name Was Ambrose

(And he's still giving away shots)

In a past issue of *The 19th Hole*, respected teaching pro, Doug Mochrie, correctly wrote that there is no such thing as a Mulligan in golf and, of course, he is right. But then he asked, "Who is this person?"

About 10 years ago I wrote one of the original articles on the history of the Mulligan for a Boston journal, so Doug's question sent me back to my own archives. First, a quote from Dick Aultman of the Golf Digest Professional Advisory Staff describes a Mulligan as "a second attempt at a shot. Usually taken on the first tee. Not recognized by the rules of golf." That's what a Mulligan is, but who is Mulligan? As the name implies and since the custom started around Boston, the Irish surely are involved.

In 1960 an uncle of mine owned the Donegal Pub in Waltham, Massachusetts. There he employed a popular bartender named Ambrose Mulligan. Often, when my uncle took a day off, Mulligan would become very generous in pouring a "drink on the house" for the regulars and occasionally would wink and say, "I think I'll take another shot for myself." Among the steady patrons at the Donegal were two golfers named Murray and Thompson. They played at the Marlboro Country Club. And after a while, whenever they hit a ball from the tee into the water or the woods, they took to saying, "I think I'll take a Mulligan." This is what another shot had become to them, a private joke, you see.

In fact, Murray often had his hand in his back pocket before his first shot fell into the pines. Of course, it was just a matter of time before this expression and illegal practice spread, first all over the Marlboro links, and then all over Massachusetts. This happened many years ago and the irony of the story is that Ambrose Mulligan himself never took up the game of golf. What happened to him? Well, he was very young when he was in Waltham and attended Northeastern University when he wasn't at the tavern working. Eventually he became an airline pilot, flying out of Los Angeles.

Ambrose Mulligan is now retired from the airlines and living in Las Vegas. I reached him by phone a few weeks ago and he reported that he still tends bar part-time and that one of these days he is going to take up golf. I like Ambrose Mulligan. When he worked at the pub back in Waltham years ago, he was a nice kid, very likable.

Did he know that one of the most popular phrases in golf was named after him? "Oh, sure. I hear it all the time when girls and guys come into the lounge, kidding each other after a round of golf. I know what it means but I never say a word. Would you? Can you imagine telling someone that you are the original Mulligan, the one that the practice was named after? Heck, they would laugh me right out of town." He went on, "Only a few close personal friends out here know the real story and they respect my privacy. In fact, I had a very hard time convincing my wife, Alice, that when she was a stewardess flying out of Minneapolis and we started going together," he said.

Ambrose said that over the years he has read or heard about other fellows named Mulligan who claim that golfing's rule-bender originated around them, and it amuses him. "I just smile and don't say a word. After all I know the real story and that's good enough for me. Hey, maybe someday I'll open my own place and you can write a story about me, and we will go public with it!"

We chatted for a few more minutes and promised to keep in touch with each other. The last thing I asked him was if he was still giving out a few free shots to the regulars? "Of course," he laughed, "You couldn't get by out here in Las Vegas without doing it I was born for this place!"

Chapter 2

Sam Snead's Advice Gone Amiss

(Sam's words send feathers flying)

While it is obvious that golf is now one of the most popular sports in the world and it seems as though everyone is playing the game, a few people wash out every year for various reasons.

A neighbor of mine, Niles, recently joined this group. When Niles first moved into our Florida retirement community a year ago, he took up golf with a dedication that was almost obsessive. Until that time he had only been to a few driving ranges in the Boston suburbs, and he proudly told me that he had dented the blade of a windmill on a fast little Cape Cod pitch and putt layout. That was his total experience with handling a club.

Once settled down here he bought new clubs and enrolled in a local golf school. He subscribed to the three major golfing magazines and watched many of the instructional videos. He studied books by Venturi, Nicklaus and Leadbetter.

Niles was out on the practice range or the course every day and was down around a 30 handicap when he hit the period of rain, thunder and lightning that comes upon Tampa Bay every summer. Bored after a few days in the house, he decided to visit the local library to browse some of the golf literature in the stacks — and this is where he ran into trouble.

Among the articles was an old interview with the legendary Sam Snead. When asked about his grip, Sam replied that he always held the club with the same amount of pressure that he would exert if he were holding a small bird in his hands. Niles, who is a nice man but a bit gullible, was really impressed by such wisdom, so much so that he decided to experience this gripping sensation himself. His wife, Dorothea, had set up an elaborate birdfeeder off their back patio and there was always activity around it. So when Niles caught a break in the daily showers, he went out back and snared an unsuspecting, small Savannah sparrow. This bird, about five inches long, felt just right in his grasp, so our neighbor went into his tee box stance, and commenced to swing and swing and swing.

Now the song of the Savannah sparrow is a series of chirps and trills, but that is only under happy conditions. When Niles became aware of a panicky shriek, he sensed that something was awry with his experiment. Certainly he had not intended to harm his little captive, but when he eased up on his grip, he was aghast at the sight of the sparrow's bulging eyeballs and apparent shortness of breath. He later confided to me that he was reminded of the sketch in his childhood nursery rhyme book, that of little bird heads sticking out of a pie.

Niles released his choke hold on the creature instantly, only to watch in horror as the unfortunate small fowl flew, in a staggered flight path, about five yards before it smashed into the pole of the very birdfeeder where he had enjoyed his breakfast that morning. Unconscious, the bird fell to the ground.

Observing this drama with great interest was Vo, a cat who lived next door to Niles and Dorothea. (Only later did Niles learn that Vo was a nickname for voracious!)

Before Niles could react, the cat snatched up the Savannah sparrow and darted into some nearby woods with his own breakfast in mind. Niles felt terrible about this rapid turn of events. Need it be said that his last sighting of the dazed warbler was the bird's accusing eyes staring at him from over Vo's shoulder as the feline and its victim vanished into the forest.

And that is the story of why Niles gave up golf.

He had trouble sleeping, often dreaming of Hitchcock's film "The Birds." Seeking relief from his guilt, he visited a church only to look up and see a mural of doves gawking at him from the ceiling.

I met Niles the other day. He has found a new activity in Sun City Center — lawnbowling. In his new uniform of white shirt and white pants he looks like a man headed for a Good Humor convention.

He claims the outdoor bowling is a great deal of fun — and he can squeeze the ball just as hard as he wants to.

Chapter 3

St. Anthony, Patron Saint of Golf

(Italian caddie makes good)

Many, many years ago when St. Anthony was a youngster in Padua, Italy, he worked as a caddie at the local country club, Padua Palms.

He was a likeable lad who also helped out in the pro shop. Of course the other kids called him Tony back then, and in time he developed a great knack for finding lost golf balls for the members. He was uncanny in this pursuit, but being a bit modest, he shyly claimed serendipity. The club pro, Mario Malatesta, said at the time, "It is almost spooky the way this kid can discover balls in the deep grass or the woods."

Young Tony had to work hard in order to help out his family, but on Mondays he was allowed to play the Palms with the other caddies. Malatesta knew the boy had some ability when he saw him hit a one iron about 220 yards, and this was centuries before Lee Trevino observed that only God could handle that club!

Eventually, Tony entered a seminary and became Anthony once again. He had an outstanding career in religion, so much so, that after his death he was canonized as St. Anthony. The church then also decreed that he would be the saint that people prayed to when looking for lost articles. You see, he could never quite shake his golf ball finding prowess, and as a young priest was terrific at helping people recover lost car keys. His reputation had spread all over Italy and even down into Sicily. Since none of the other saints were interested in golf, it was almost an afterthought that the Vatican also named him Patron Saint of Golf.

Here the reader might wonder just what all this has to do with him and his game in today's world of golf. Let us explain. We have learned through reliable sources, and it was very, very difficult, that after arriving at heaven's Elysian fairways and greens, St. Anthony started spending a lot of his time in the putting department. He has come to consider it his own special province, and he takes a very unusual interest in what goes on there.

St. Anthony considers putting quite different from the rest of the game. In fact, it was he who first observed with sagacious remark that, "in the art of putting it is always wise to keep the ball on the ground!" Very early every morning a seraph angel checks into the office with a long list of golfer's names and their tee times for courses all over the world down below. As each name is read aloud, St. Anthony shakes his head either "yes" or "no" and that's it for the day.

If the seraph says "McGinley's golfing today down in Sun City Center, Florida" and St. Anthony says "no" then we won't make a putt all day. But if it's "yes" I can't miss! A friend, Fr. Tucker, who has an early service for Sunday morning golfers in Litchfield, Connecticut, took a special interest when we told him this story, as his parish is named St. Anthony of Padua. So we decided after talking with him, that a prayer in the form of a poem might be appropriate, thus we composed the following.

A Golfer's Prayer
To St. Anthony

If this ball goes slicing,
into the woods today,
It's you, St. Anthony, we ask,
please locate it right away.
And once on the green
help us to find the hole
With a nice, easy stroke
and a sure, accurate roll.
Because you're the finder
when things go wrong,
So, please, St. Anthony
pay attention to our song!

Chapter 4

A Slight Distraction

(Nice to have someone
show you the course)

Years ago, late in the afternoon outside Des Moines, Iowa, I checked into a motel and went out to try to get in nine holes at a local golf course, taking advantage of daylight-saving time.

As I signed in, the assistant pro asked me if I might be paired with a local old timer called Whitey, who was looking for a game. Since I was happy for some company who would know his way around the links, I agreed.

Whitey was a nice, old man, and we chatted as we pulled our carts down the fairway. It wasn't until we arrived on the green of the second hole that a strange phenomenon left me agape.

I had a four-foot putt to the cup, while Whitey faced a seven footer, so he was away. He made a nice stroke, but the putt broke left, a few inches from the hole. He then rolled his eyes upward to heaven in such a strange manner that the pupils disappeared.

I was left staring at the full whites of his eyes! And they remained that way! I didn't want to embarrass my new friend, so I attempted my putt and jerked it three feet past the cup. Whitey then muttered something inaudible. "What?" I asked. "Please hit me on the back of the head," he requested. I did. His eyes descended to their proper position, and we went on with the game.

Since Whitey didn't offer any explanation, I avoided mentioning the incident. But it's really hard to putt when the person across the green puts such a gaze upon you. It was like looking at a pair of egg whites, so I prayed that it wouldn't happen again. No such luck. Again on the fifth green the eyes went up and refused to budge. Again the plaintive request, "Please hit me on the back of the head." And again it occurred on the seventh hole, and finally on the finishing (thank goodness!) ninth green. As we made our way to the clubhouse, Whitey asked me if I might join him for dinner that night, but I excused myself, explaining that I had some phone calls to make from my motel room. I just couldn't see myself banging old Whitey on the back of the head in a crowded restaurant, so we parted company.

After that second hole, I didn't have to ask why they called him Whitey!

Chapter 5

The Range Ball

(Finders, keepers)

I was over at the driving range the other day working on a few clubs. Our range has an automatic ball dispensing machine and after you pay $3 at the pro shop you receive a token to place in the slot of the unit and out comes 35 or 40 range balls. Sometimes, just before inserting the medallion, if you give the machine a little body check in the manner of a hockey defenseman, you might get a few more balls.

After the pail filled up I went over to the area roped off for hitting and emptied the balls on the ground. Usually I don't count the balls, but sometimes I lay them out in rows of eight if I am working on five specific clubs. These balls, being range balls, are pretty beat up, but low and behold, there among these veterans stood out a brand new Titleist No. 3. I couldn't believe my good luck, but later on, the more I thought about it, the more I think I figured out just what happened to bring about this serendipity.

Some poor golfer, not unlike myself, saw an ad in one of the magazines that guaranteed that if he would send them about $500, they would deliver to his house a new bubble, titanium or precious metal driver that would not only add 20 yards to his drives, but would eliminate his slice ad infinitum! Since our friend's tee shot averaged about 180 yards, he got all excited and immediately phoned in his order, with an extra $10 for delivery within two days. When the new club arrived, he rushed over to the range and started whacking balls like mad!

He warmed up with a 7 iron and then went to his brand new miracle driver (which wouldn't be a bad name to use in the ad—The Miracle Driver—a miracle if you get 20 more yards!). And he did seem to gain distance right away, perhaps eight or 10 yards, he estimated. Then the thought struck him, what if he really let loose with a brand new ball instead of the very fatigued range offerings? How far would it soar? He didn't waste a second as he reached into his bag and retrieved the sparkling Titleist No. 3 ball. I like to think that he hit it a ton out there into the hundreds of balls resting on the range field and went home tickled pink with his new driver.

And that's the story of the nice new Titleist coming into my possession.

Thank you, new found friend.

That should be the end of the story, except that a day or so later, on a water hole at our course, I hooked my unexpected find right into a deep six, Titanic-type watery demise!

I love these new floating golf balls.

Chapter 6

Sand Wedge Or Sand Hog

"When in the sand and about to use your wedge, imagine that you are spooning coffee. That should do it."

—A. George Gilman
Salem Country Club
Peabody, Mass. (Circa 1948)

The old Squire, Gene Sarazen, invented the sand wedge club in 1932 in New Port Richey, Florida and used it to win both the U.S. and British Opens. This old iron has been a hard working stiff ever since. I have a fine one that cost me $30.

The latest, up-to-date technology drivers cost well over $500 and are made of titanium. A golfer knows what a driver is for and when he should employ the sand wedge, but where do these two stand in the food chain of your golf bag? Here is some comparative information to mull over:

• On a football team the titanium driver would play quarterback; the sand wedge, a down-and-dirty nose tackle.

• For transportation the titanium driver would be given a stretch limo; the sand wedge would ride the subway.

• Career wise the titanium driver would be with Merrill Lynch on Wall Street, while the sand wedge would build water tunnels 300 feet under Times Square.

• Educationally, the titanium driver would be accepted by Princeton University; the sand wedge would work its way through City College of New York.

• In reading selections, the titanium driver would be at home with Goldsmith's "The Deserted Village"; the sand wedge would recite "The Cremation of Sam McGee" by Robert Service.

• For overnight accommodations the titanium driver would stay at The Plaza near Central Park. The sand wedge would be quite at home in a Red Roof Inn over in Queens.

Talk to the golf ball as it flies through the air, but do not converse with the sand wedge, it's busy and has a job to do. Do not distract it. A whispered "Thank you" will suffice after a bunker rescue.

And beware, a titanium driver can get you into a lot of trouble but it's the sand wedge that will usually bail you out!

Chapter 7

Who Are We Playing, Coach?

(A sport much harder than golf,
if you can't swim)

The great Bobby Jones lamented once that in playing in a golf tournament you are on your own, because many times you don't even see your opponent. He was comparing the situation to other sports where you are engaged in competition with someone only a few feet from you, such as boxing, football or basketball. Also in golf, physical pain is usually self-inflicted. In fact, in golf the only real pain that I ever felt was in the clubhouse where I sprained my wrist dealing cards in a pitch game.

In boxing the other person who is trying to punch you out is just a foot or so away. While wrestling, the other fellow's sweat and body odor pinned me before he did. But in the first three days of the U.S. Open or the Masters, the players have to search out the leader board to stay current with the parade of events. They say that Ben Hogan focused so much on his game, that he wasn't even aware of what was going on in his own foursome.

Which brings to mind, my own personal all-time worst experience with an opponent. Though I could hardly dog-paddle, I was conned into a water polo game at a pool in Edina, Minnesota, many years ago, as one of the teams was shorthanded. In 15 feet of water the ball came to me and I was immediately taken from behind in a choke hold. I went down about five feet where I gave up the ball, as I was scratched and kneed in a sensitive area. I lost consciousness, but fortunately the referee, who was a lifeguard, hauled me out of the pool.

After resuscitation and with the water out of my lungs, I lay poolside still reviving. I then heard a tiny voice ask, "Are you all right, mister?" I looked up into the sun and beheld a small girl, about eight years old and maybe 70 pounds, anxiously hovering over me. "I'm sorry that I got carried away out there. I didn't mean to drown you like that," she said.

And that was the termination of my water polo career, throttled by an eight-year-old future Olympian, who though diminutive, had very sharp fingernails. I'll take the fairways anytime, whether I see the other guy or not!

Chapter 8

You Had To Be There

(A little fun on a hot afternoon)

On a hot "up the lazy river" summer day, a friend and I were playing at Stow Acres Golf Course, outside of Boston.

Up until a few years ago this 36-hole facility was one of the few remaining layouts in the country that did not allow gas or electric golf carts. You had to carry your bag or use a pull cart. This course made the Golf Digest top 75 list continuously.

My pal, Dick Andrews, and I had played old-timer hockey and softball together in nearby Sudbury. There weren't many playing out on the links that afternoon. It was peaceful and the course was in repose. Since there was just the two of us, we played a casual game, not adhering strictly to the rules of golf.

We were finishing on the South Course at Stow. The 18th hole is a long 507-yard par 5 dogleg left, with a good-sized pond about 150 yards in front of an elevated tee.

Since it's hard to carry the water from the tee, you can go either right or left to get around the lagoon. With Dick's first shot, a brand new Titleist landed in the fairway to the right. After I hit to the right, Dick said that he'd like to take a Mulligan, an extra shot, to see if he could take a short cut down the left side.

So he did, and his shot came out exactly as he had planned. This left him with a ball on each side of the water. He then said that he would play the shot on the left, as he did not get into that area too often. He asked me to pick up his brand new Titleist.

I said, "Fine," and as I was getting near his ball I slipped an old practice ball that was very clean from my bag. When I got to his Titleist I made the switch and yelled over the pond to him, "Hey, Dick, I'll hit your ball over to you." "No, no!" he started to scream, but before he could finish his plea I deliberately chunked a 9 iron shot into the lake. "Sorry, Dick," I said. "It got away from me."

It got real quiet out there. I waited the appropriate amount of time before

I let him off the hook, holding up his Titleist for him to see. "Boy," he said. "You really set me up. Let's finish this hole so we can get into the 19th. I could use a cold one!"

THE RIGHT TIME OF THE DAY

Two old veterans were playing with a novice golfer on a hole that ran alongside a road. On a 150 yard par three, one of the old timers hooked his drive out onto the street where it hit the side of a school bus and rebounded back onto the course, rolling across the green, and halting six inches from the cup. "How in the world did you ever do that?" asked the startled rookie. "You have to know the bus schedule," was the laconic reply!

Chapter 9

Down East

(In a way, the clubhouse at a golf course should be like your home, with lots of love and laughter there, if you don't have that — you are just camping out!)

If you go into any of the major bookstores at your local mall and check out the golf section, you will find that there are at least three or four books being sold that contain humorous quotes from various past and present touring golf professionals.

Each publication carries quite a few remarks made over the years by Chi Chi Rodriguez and Lee Trevino. These two guys are very funny and their observations usually get everyone's attention, especially the print media.

Humor is a very integral part of the golf scene, and amateurs are just as capable of coming up with some funny lines, out on the course or in the clubhouse. My wife, Carolee, and I spent 10 days this spring in New England, primarily to attend a wedding, but I was able to get in four rounds of golf in Massachusetts and Connecticut.

The first story happened at the McGinley Open held once a year at the Wampanoag Country Club in West Hartford, where my brothers, sons and various nephews gather each year to establish bragging rights for the season. In the pro shop on a counter was a dish with wooden tees in it for the members. Since my nephew, Mark, qualifies, he stuck his big paw in there and hauled out a fistful of tees. "Hey, Mark," the assistant pro cried, "What are you building, a house?" "Yeah" answered the nephew, showing unusual mental alacrity for a McGinley, "A tea house!"

The next incident I walked into was a week later at the Sagamore Spring Golf Course in Lynnfield, Massachusetts. Rain delayed our tee time and we were sitting in the coffee shop chatting with a group from DeAngelo's Barber Shop in nearby Malden. After awhile one of their foursome got tired of waiting and headed for the door. "This rain's not going to stop. I'm heading home," he said. "No, no" the other guys yelled, but he insisted. He stood in the doorway and bid his pals adieu with this remark: "I would much rather lose a golf match in the sunshine than win one in the pouring rain!" After the hoots and howls died down, everyone agreed that this chap was indeed a fair weather golfer.

This final tale comes out of western Massachusetts where two salesmen had knocked off work early one afternoon to get in a round at a local nine-hole course. Next to the layout was an ancient cemetery where one of the guys hooked his drive over a stone fence, out of bounds, into the graveyard.

Going onto the sacred ground, he spotted his ball resting between two plots. He noticed that the stones had the same last names, a husband and wife in a family grave. Curious, he read the inscription on the stone nearest his ball. It said: "Finally, Thou Hast Ceased Snoring."

• • •

Here's a story that may top all clubhouse stories. Every year on or about Aug. 15th I start sneezing as the ragweed and goldenrod come to life. My golfing companions are used to seeing me out on the fairways with a few handkerchiefs in hand. Lately, with the new sprays it's not too bad, but up in New England a few years ago, it was uncomfortable.

One afternoon when we were back in the clubhouse, six or seven guys were sitting around a table for refreshments at Stow Acres in Stow, Massachusetts, and one of the group was bragging a bit too much about the great round that he had shot. I was sitting next to him, and a few feet behind us there was a water cooler against the wall. I took out a handkerchief, went over to the cooler and filled a paper cup, all behind his back. I crept back, dipped two fingers into the water (by now some of the other golfers were watching me), faked a loud "ahh choo," and flipped the water on my unsuspecting victim's neck. I then innocently whispered in his ear, "Sorry, did I get you?" Wow! What a response I got. "DID YOU GET ME?... DID YOU GET ME?" it usually starts out.

Of course by that time, everyone else around the table was in stitches. I then finished with the clumsy attempt to wipe off his neck and ear area with one of my handkerchiefs, and it usually takes the guy a few minutes to catch on to the ruse. One thing though that we must be careful about, when you deliver the spray, don't get too close to the victim, as sometimes they shoot right up in the air, or else they go rigid and freeze like a St. Paul Winter Carnival ice statue. The reactions seem to vary over the years!

Chapter 10

Let Us Count The Ways

(How doesn't matter, as long as it's in)

In his book, "Golf My Way," Jack Nicklaus has a great section on putting. He writes that he likes to topple the ball into the hole, calling himself a "die" putter. Jack then describes Arnold Palmer as a "charge" putter, one who bangs the ball into the back of the cup hard enough to trap it there.

These insightful observations inspired us to start counting the many ways that a golf ball can enter the hole at the end of it's short or long journey. We started a list and here is where we are at this writing:

• The ball can plunge into the hole like a skydiver whose chute is reluctant to unfurl.

• It can crawl into the cup like your neighbor coming home at 3 am.

• The ball can swagger into the hole like John Wayne entering the swinging doors of Rose's Cantina in El Paso.

• It can skip into the cup like Richard Simmons leading his exercise group.

• The ball may plummet into the hole similar to the FAA description of a plane crash as, "a controlled flight into terrain." Sounds like a hole in one!

• It can plop into the cup like a cow splattering the floor of the barn.

• The ball can stumble into the hole like Red Skelton doing a skit in an antique shop.

• It can tumble into the cup like a scuba diver going overboard backward into the sea.

Oh, the latest way the ball can fall: When a putter like Arnold bangs the back of the cup and the ball goes up in the air about two inches and drops back in — it's a Michael Jordan!

We have observed the darn thing lurch, dive, slide and perform a dozen other rather theatrical arrivals around the sometimes pouting lips of the cup. My own putts? Well, they have been described as collapsing into the place, where the ball seeks the deepening shade and finds midnight, as I myself am ready to collapse after a three-foot downhill, breaking tap, goes down.

Now, in conclusion, how many ways can a ball go <u>by</u> the hole on the green? I'm not ready to write about that scene yet, it's just too negative an exercise!

Right Under Your Nose

In our home whenever we lose something, my wife says, "Look around; it doesn't have legs, it can't walk away." So we weren't surprised when the results of a survey among local golfers showed that 50 percent of the time, when they thought they had left a club back on a previously played hole, it was still in their bag!

Chapter 11

Hey, It's Your Golf Ball

(That's what family is all about)

The golf pro Lee Trevino made one of his profound observations about the game a while back when he commented, "You can talk to a fade, but a hook won't listen."

After reading that remark the thought descended upon me that golf is one of those rare games where you actually own the ball. You paid for it, you furnished it transportation, and you housed it, either in your garage or bedroom, and finally, into your bag.

In baseball you do not own the ball. In fact, a baseball spends most of its brief career deep in the umpires' pockets. It develops only a short union with the pitcher or catcher and other players.

In fact, the batter is trying his utmost to actually make the old apple vanish over the outfield fence.

In golf this would be a calamity, as a lost ball calls for an immediate search before the match can continue.

Other major sports such as football and basketball do not put up with ball ownership. The fan may think that Michael Jordan owns the ball or Dan Marino has his own football, but it just looks that way because they seem to control these objects so much of the time. They do not have a clear deed or title.

Years ago the Detroit Tigers had a fine young hurler named Mark Fidrych. He caused a great deal of excitement in the American League when he was seen talking to the baseball. He admitted to the custom and it's a shame that the dialogue was never recorded.

So, why not talk to your golf ball? It's yours, you own it and you should give it preflight encouragement. Nourish it, console it, and, after one goes astray, as a good ball will sometimes do, welcome it back when you locate it, with kind and non-judgmental empathy. Believe me you will play a much better game with this new attitude.

And Fidrych, what happened to him? Well, he hurt his arm and had to retire early from baseball to Northborough, Massachusetts. There, he farms and has a fleet of trucks. He doesn't talk to baseballs anymore, but recently was seen in an intense conversation with his steering wheel - as we all frequently do!

"You can talk to a fade,
but a hook won't listen!"

—Lee Trevino

"You can yell at thunder,
but lightning is deaf!"

—T. McG

Stormy Weather

The Tampa Bay area is generally regarded as the lightning capital of the country. In fact, the rumor is that when Phil Esposito came down here from N.Y. to get a hockey team established, he did not have any trouble in naming the club the Tampa Bay Lightning.

So when we read the famous quote on the previous page by Lee Trevino, who likes to talk out on the course, it reminded us that he had suffered a terrible back injury when he and several other players were struck by lightning in Chicago years ago.

We have written in the past that when playing in weather that might turn bad, make sure you have a tall partner, and never, never play with someone with a name like Tommy Bolt!

But lightning is a pretty serious matter here in Florida out on a golf course, and we have noticed that more and more players are getting off the links when they suspect that this tool of nature's wrath is anywhere near them. So, when you hear that thunder, don't wait to see any flashes or bolts, get off the fairway, and take refuge in the clubhouse — pronto.

Chapter 12

Golf In The Real Kingdom

(What a few old friends are doing now)

When I read in the Golf Digest a few years back that Michael Murphy had written a book entitled "Golf in the Kingdom" the thought struck me — finally somebody had the temerity and curiosity to address a question that we have heard many times over the years on the tee, or, in the locker room. When a golfer, looking ahead down the road, chuckling nervously, raised the question, "Do you think that golf is played up in heaven?"

Although a terrific read, Murphy's work was more about an international golfing experience rather than spiritual. So the question is still out there to ponder because we have observed that while the inquiry is always raised in a joking manner, it is also hopefully phrased. And yet, who could answer such a question? We have had one train of thought that at least gets the investigation under way.

In the Old Testament, people were quite often, while asleep, subject to visions where other folks revealed startling information to them about something important, and generally these images were quite stern in pronouncing behavior. I mean that you probably did not get much of an opportunity to question them about anything at all. You would probably be shaking and stammering something like "But, but-" and get a stern warning such as "Be quiet; I do all the talking in this phantasm!" After their disclosure, off they would go into the bright, blinding light that always seems to be available for their dramatic departure.

I have two golfers that we would like to speak with under such conditions with a chance for inquiry, and one of them actually passed away out on the course. Bing Crosby, the famous singer and movie actor, died of a massive heart attack on the 18th, and really final for him, hole at La Moralejo Golf Club outside Madrid, Spain. The date was Oct. 14, 1977 and we know that for sure, because a man I play with, Ed Rudolphy of Sun City Center, Florida, was on the 17th fairway of the course at the time. As you can imagine, all heck broke loose. An odd twist to Bing's demise is that his wife, Katherine, arranged for an old fashioned Irish wake for der Bingle. She rented an entire floor in a west Los Angeles hotel and invited all Bing's golfing buddies, led by Phil Harris, an old ball striker who really liked the south!

Why do we feel that the popular crooner has attained eternal salvation? Well, in this case we apply the Latin phrase, "De Mortuis Nil Nisi Bonum," (say nothing but good of the dead) and after all, the management up there would never pass up the opportunity to have Bing Crosby sing "Silent Night" for them.

Awhile back, a close friend and golfing companion for many years, Al LaFreniere, brought up the subject of golf in the Promised Land while we were waiting on a tee for a group in front of us. "Well, I certainly hope that they have golf in heaven because I have already played in the inferno and it isn't much fun!" Al explained that during his career in the Foreign Service he had played golf in the United Arab Emirates, near Abu Dhabi in the desert, where temperatures would run up to 120 degrees quite often. What number sun block lotion?

There is another departed golfer that we really would love to visit with once more. He was a "Townie" from Charlestown, Mass., born in the shadow of Bunker Hill, and his name was Fr. Jack Hartigan. "Townies" in Boston are a special breed, as the Oakland Raider turned announcer, Howie Long, will attest.

After seeing hard action in the Pacific in World War II, Fr. Jack studied at Boston College and then entered the seminary as a late vocation. After several assignments in parish work he became a chaplain for the Massachusetts State Police and also pastored Our Lady of Fatima Church in Sudbury, Massachusetts, where we met him. He worked very hard but also loved to play golf and fish. He was a member of the Framingham Golf Club and played up in Lake Sunapee, New Hampshire, at a course where Gene Sarazen often visited in the summer. He was about a 14-15 handicap.

Why do we think that Fr. Hartigan could give us some insight as to what goes on golfwise in the Promised Land? Well, not because of the religious connection as you might think, but because we do feel that the man had an edge. You see, at Framingham over the years, he had three aces. Quite a feat. After he passed away we were pleased to be involved in the first few Fr. Hartigan Memorial Golf Tournaments in the Sudbury area. He was a wonderful man.

So perhaps Fr. Jack, Bobby Jones and Bing Crosby are playing the lush Seraphim Country Club, and just maybe, Tony Lema, has found three holes that he can once again christen Amen Corner, as he did at the Masters. And a recent arrival named Ben Hogan will surely join them. Ben, always in his dreams, sought to play the perfect round of golf, a hole in one on every hole, a score of 18. He has the reputation of being the hardest worker in golf, so we hope that his dream comes true, because only up there, could it happen!

The Lift, Wipe And Place Rule

In 1988, when the Honda Classic was being played at Eagle Trace, Brad Faxon watched his first tee shot vanish from the middle of the fairway. A seagull sped down, picked up his ball in its beak and dropped it in a water hazard some 50 yards away. Faxon, however, was given a break. Rules officials allowed him to drop at his original lie.

The above note in the Golf Section of the *Tampa Tribune* by their capable writer, Mick Elliott, reminds us of a letter we received at *The Observer News* a few years back inquiring about handling a situation on the green of a course quite near the bay, where a seagull had soiled upon a ball resting there. We advised the reader that because the green was so close to the water, there is probably a local rule in conjunction with Cleaning Ball Rule #21 of the USGA Rules that would allow the use of toilet paper or a handkerchief in washing the ball. As for the seagull, he (and it seems like something the male would do) would probably take off for the Sunshine Skyway Bridge before you could render him any assistance!

Clearly, Four Nonfictitious Essays

One Sad .... (Ben Hogan)

One Inspiring .... (The Bauer Family)

One Jocular .... (Jack and Me)

One Courageous .... (Gordy Schilling)

Chapter 13

Ben Hogan, The Wee Ice Man

(The child is father of the man)

Two Serious Articles

Although the majority of articles and essays in this book are a blend of fiction and non-fictitious happenings, the next two stories are about two PGA pros, generations apart, and the tragedies that struck them in different ways.

The first piece is about the legendary Ben Hogan and how his career was possibly influenced by the suicide of his father. The second work tells of teaching pro John Bauer and his sudden passing, affecting his wife, Chris, and daughter, Beth, who is the top female amateur golfer in the country.

The odd coincidence is that we met Ben Hogan many years ago and Chris and Beth Bauer have become personal friends to Carolee and me, and we are delighted to know them.

•••••

About 1950, my brother Joe and I were following Sam Snead and the Ryder Cup team around the Belmont Country Club in Belmont, Massachusetts, when we noticed Ben Hogan standing alone under a tree near us.

Hogan, one of the best golfers ever, was recovering from the terrible automobile accident involving a Greyhound bus that almost killed him and his wife, Valerie. He was the non-playing captain of the Ryder contingent that year, and he told us that he was walking the course to get his legs back in shape.

The man that the Scots christened the "Wee Ice Man" was quiet and polite as he autographed our programs.

Those legs recovered enough to carry this diminutive 130-pound shotmaker on to win the U.S Open, the Masters and British Open over the next three years.

Ben Hogan was quite reserved and taciturn, but those few closest to him spoke of his warm heart and acute sense of humor. Unlike the well-published comments of Lee Trevino and Chi Chi Rodriguez, quotes by

Hogan are rarely found in golf books or journals. More like him is the conversation he had with Ken Venturi after he took a seven on the initial hole of a match. Venturi said, as they walked off the green, "Tough hole, Ben." Hogan looked him in the eye and replied, "That's why we play 18." He then went on to shoot a 69.

When Ben Hogan was nine years old, he was in a room in a house in Dublin, Texas, when his father, Chester, a blacksmith, committed suicide with a pistol. This surely had much to do with the demeanor that the boy assumed for the years ahead.

The family moved to Fort Worth where Ben discovered the game of golf, as a caddy. After work, he practiced alone every day until dark in an unusual, driving dedication to perfection.

Over the years his hard work paid off, and he achieved legendary status. Perhaps, because of the enormous, disturbing effect that his dad's death had upon him, he was quietly determined to establish the family name in a good light.

Today you will see the name Hogan on golf balls, hats, and clubs all over the world. There is even a Hogan tour for young, aspiring players.

Ben Hogan's image on a golf course was marked by an enduring air and a focused concentration. He coolly stared forward, then executed a perfect shot.

His own death was not easy, as he spent his last months with complications of cancer and Alzheimer's. We are reminded of a line from the poem, Thomas Gray's "Elegy Written in a Country Churchyard": "And Melancholy marked him for her own."

Chapter 14

Remembered Affectionately, A Teaching Pro

(John and Chris, then Beth, and the beat goes on)

"And love is how you stay alive,
even after you are gone."
—Prof. Morrie Schwartz, Brandeis University
(From the current Mitch Albom book, "Tuesdays With Morrie")

Up on U.S. 301, a few miles north of Sun City Center, Florida, is the Summerfield Golf Course, part of the community of Summerfield Crossings.

Out on the 16th hole there is a permanent memorial rock with a plaque that reads "In memory of John Bauer" and under that, "The Wind Beneath Beth's Wings."

The 16th was John's favorite hole. Beth is his daughter.

John Bauer left Illinois with his attractive wife, Chris, around 1978. He had been a college football and baseball standout at Illinois State in Normal, Illinois. (In American Legion ball he once hurled a no-hitter.)

It was his golf game, though, that drew this couple to Florida. John spent about 11 years at the Airco course in Clearwater, working on all phases of the game. Daughter Beth was born in Largo.

People at Airco still fondly remember the PGA pro. The description heard most often: "He always had a smile on his face." One of his former employees enthused, "He was just wonderful, the best boss that I ever had anywhere."

I ran into similar comments later at Crescent Oaks in Palm Harbor, the next stop in John's career. It became apparent to me that John Bauer was a young man with an educated heart.

Perry Payne, the superintendent at Crescent Oaks, said John was "one of the most likeable individuals that I ever met."

Eventually, another offer came along, and John, Christine and Beth moved to the Summerfield course, where the golfer assumed a general managership. The people at Crescent Oaks were understandably very disappointed.

As Beth grew, so did her golf game... with Dad's coaching. Three years ago, she attracted local and national attention in golfing circles when, at 13, she took her first American Junior Title in the upper level 14-18 age group.

Victories have accumulated ever since, and to date the Bloomingdale High School senior has chalked up 26 national junior wins. She is a three-time Florida girls high school champ and four-time Junior All-American. Tragedy struck the young family swiftly and unexpectedly in 1994. John Bauer, at 41 years of age, was struck down by the fatal Guillain-Barre syndrome, a painful neurological disease that took his life in three short weeks.

Beth had just won the PGA Junior Championship, an accomplishment she was able to share with her mom and dad just before his death.

Now, with the help of her supportive mother, Beth has been able to carry her career forward. She said she knows that her dad is with her always.

Her new coach, Phil Krick, was mainly concerned whether he could carry on the good work that John had fostered. He has evidently done a fine job.

Craig Morissette, a former college golfer and current manager at the Summerfield course, said that Beth has the ability and the desire, plus a good head for the game. She and her mom are evaluating quite a few college offers these days, but the LPGA is the long-range goal. Beth's future is very bright.

About now, Beth is in Spain as a guest of the Ryder Cup squad. There she will again meet her friend, Davis Love III, who also lost his teaching-pro father. His dad died in a plane crash.

It is said that you can observe the famed Rock of Gibraltar about eight miles off the coast, from the Valderrama course where the matches are being played. It might remind Beth Bauer that she has a rock of her own back at the 16th hole of the Summerfield links, where she always pays personal respects to her dad.

Mark Twain penned some words that would apply very comfortably to John Bauer. "Praise is well, compliment is well, but affection, that is the last, and final and most precious reward that any man can win."

John Bauer surely merited his share of that response from everyone he touched!

After having received scholarship offers from colleges all over the United States, Beth Bauer will start at Duke University in Durham, N.C. in Sept. 1998. In February of this year she was honored by the Tampa Sports Club with their prestigious Florida Sports Personality Award. Past winners list many of the well-known names in the sports world, such as Pete Sampras in tennis, Lou Piniella in baseball, and Don Shula and Steve Spurrier of football fame.

Below is her golfing record as of March 1998.

- 5-time American Junior Golf Association All American
- 26 National Junior victories
- Only female (and third golfer) to win back-to-back AJGA Tournament of Champions
- One of only four players in AJGA history to win both Tournament of Champions (Stroke Play) and Rolex Jr. Classic (Match Play) in same year.
- 3 time Florida Girls High School State Champion
- One of 12 Juniors (six girls, six boys) selected to compete against Europe in Ryder Cup Preliminary Match in Spain.
- Ranked number one in U.S. Junior Girls and PGA Juniors
- Named 1997 American Junior Golf Association Player of the Year
- People's Choice for 1997 top Female Amateur Athlete
- Finished the prestigious Nabisco Dinah Shore major tied for 15th slot with LPGA pro Meg Mallon at Rancho Mirage, California. She shot a 76-70-72-72 on the tough Shore tournament course and was lowest among the several other amateurs that were invited. She also out-performed many veteran participants. For a teenager still in high school this was an outstanding performance.

As this book is going to press, we did not think that Tod would mind if we inserted this information. Beth, playing on an amateur exemption, just competed in the U.S. Open at Kohler, Wisconsin, and was a contributing member of the U.S. Curtis Cup team that defeated the English and Irish women golfers at the Minikahda Club in Minneapolis. (We follow Beth Bauer also!

M&M Printing

Here we are at the All Star Cafe in Orlando, Florida, when Beth was indoctrinated into the Florida Hall of Fame. Her mom, Chris Bauer, is pictured at left, myself, and Beth Bauer on the right.

Chapter 15

Jack And Me

(A few words with the game's greatest)

I would have never met Jack Nicklaus if it hadn't been for a friend, Dick Schnittker, a former Ohio State basketball and football star and Minneapolis Laker, who came from Kelleys Island in Lake Erie, off Sandusky, Ohio.

Dick and I worked together for the H.B. Fuller Co. of St. Paul, Minn., and we were in Las Vegas for a national sales meeting. We were crossing the lounge at the Sahara after a Don Rickles show, and since Dick was about 6'5", he was easy to spot when someone hailed him from across the room. It was Jack Nicklaus. He and another alum from Ohio State, who I believe was a quarterback on a squad with Schnittker, were on their way to a golf tournament in California.

Now I have told this story to fellow golfers many times over the years. Jack bought the four of us a round of drinks, (Did I just write that I was in a foursome that included Jack Nicklaus!). We then chatted for five or 10 minutes, but over the years I have naturally increased that time, and we are now approaching about one hour! Anyway, while Schnittker recalled gridiron war stories with the signal caller, Jack politely asked me what sports I might have participated in. We replied that we had played a lot of ice hockey in school and after in Massachusetts and Minnesota, and a fair amount of golf. Nicklaus nodded and then commented that he and his fellow pros believed that golf was the toughest game in the world. I laughed and said, "Jack, I have to ask you a question." "What's that?" he said. "How many stitches did you ever take out on a golf course?" He got a big kick out of that, chuckled, and said, "Aw, you know what I mean." Of course he meant that golf is the hardest game in the world, right up there with playing water polo if you can't swim! We have since found out just what the game's greatest player meant that night in Las Vegas when he said how hard golf was, Jack himself wrote in his excellent book, "My Way," that the game is "imperfectable." Boy, he got that right!

How many years ago did Dick Schnittker and I bump into Nicklaus and his friend? Well, I guess it was around 1967, as there were some Green Bay Packers in the lounge, coming back from the first Super Bowl in Los

Angeles where they had beaten Kansas City. Dick was living in Green Bay at the time, and knew a few of the guys and had played golf at the Oneida course with Coach Vince Lombardi. We have been following the career of Jack Nicklaus ever since. Dick Schnittker is out in Arizona now and we have been in Florida for five years. I understand that Jack Nicklaus lives over on the Florida East Coast; perhaps we'll bump into him again somewhere. Maybe he will allow me to buy the round this time!

Chapter 16

Schilling's Successful Swing

(A handicap? What's that?)

Along the scenic banks of the Manatee River, on the golf course once called The Moorings, a fellow named Gordon Schilling hit a hole-in-one on the Par 3, second hole, a few weeks ago.

Many people play all their life and never score an ace. In this case, the event is exceptionally special because the right handed Gordy Schilling has only one arm! The former Honeywell manager from Edina, Minn. lost his left arm in an automobile accident back in 1942.

Gordy's friends refer to him affectionately as the "one arm bandit," — a name he, himself employs in conversations. There's probably a double meaning in this description as Schilling is a pretty good ball striker and shot an 88 at Manatee awhile back, possibly taking some change from someone.

The hole where he got his first ace is 165 yards long and he estimates that his shot traveled about 140 yards from the front of the tee. There is water in front of the tees and the dance floor is well trapped with bunkers on each side and in the rear. Gordy's great shot had plenty of witnesses, as he was with three foursomes, and his very nice wife, Marylyn, was in the quartet right behind him. Needless to say there was a lot of shouting and yelling going back and forth out there.

In our visit with him, Gordy, who has been playing golf for many years, says that he has never heard of another one arm person scoring an ace, nor have I. Also, on the very next day after his exciting experience, and on the same # 2 hole, he wedged a fantastic sand shot from the bunker into the cup, for a birdie two. In the club's annual men's championship, he was low net champion in his division.

So if you are thinking about playing that nice golf layout down at Manatee, off U.S. 41, south of Ruskin, you just might need Gordon Schilling's permission to play the second hole there. As Marylyn would attest, Gordy owns it!

Chapter 17

For Sale: A Hole In One

(So what? Take it and run)

At the Oak Hill course in Rochester, N.Y. in 1989, during the U.S. Open and on the par 3 sixth hole, four professionals on the same day, got aces with shots of 175 yards to the green. They are Nick Price, Jerry Pate, Doug Weaver and Mark Wiebe. They weren't in the same foursome but someone later remarked that "It was hard not for the ball to go in!"

The second shot of Gene Sarazen's double eagle 2 on the 485 yard par 5, 15th hole in the 1935 Masters ranks right up there as one of the most exciting moments in golfing history. But for the average Joe, a hole in one is the perfect score that is always in his dreams.

We look forward to that experience, and in our pursuit of it, will keep swinging until we can't make the turn anymore. The majority of aces in modern play are showing up on par 3s and on little longer, executive layouts. This is simply because a regulation facility has only four par 3 holes, so there is less opportunity as there might be on an executive that probably features 13 or 14 chances.

This book is not to denigrate the actual event itself and it's a wonderful experience to be out there with someone who has been only playing for a year or so and see how excited they get when the ball lands on the green and finds the cup. I will take one of those any time, any place.

But some of the managers of the retirement golfing operations in the South are sometimes a little aggressive in almost guaranteeing a hole in one if you build a house in their development. A few years ago this story came out of the strip on the Atlantic that has so many courses between Myrtle Beach and Hilton Head, South Carolina.

It seems that a development had a 27 hole course on their tract of land and water and the vice president of sales set up an arrangement with the head greenskeeper that he would slope a few of the par 3 holes to channel the ball toward the cup. He promised the man that he would get a cash bonus for every ace registered in the clubhouse. They would meet every few weeks in a local tavern and settle up. Of course, eventually greed reared its ugly head and the superintendent went too far.

There were aces made almost every day. The members of the course were going crazy and hole in one parties abounded. The sales manager called the greenskeeper for a meeting. They had an argument and ended up rolling around on the floor of the pub, to the amusement of the other patrons. It seems the straw that broke the camel's back was when a local paper reported that a six-year-old girl, who was left handed, got an ace on a 130 yard hole, using the back of her grandmother's blade putter to make the swing.

The matter was corrected when the sales V.P. got the owner of the project to terminate the greenkeeper and a consultant came in to help redesign the holes in question. Gosh, I wish I had a chance to get up there before that happened!

Chapter 18

Golfers Nurture Rare Orchids

(Unusual Garden on Wauchula Course)

We have never been to Wauchula, Florida, but I am attracted to the lyrical sound of the name, it has a nice ring to it, Wauchula.. .Wauchula... and as Vaughn Monroe crooned, "There I've said it again."

We only know a few things about the town. It is where the august and venerable sportswriter of the Tampa Tribune, Tom McEwen, was raised and, a few years ago a magazine out of Bradenton named the town "the love bug capital of Florida." But recently a golf story came out of this area that, though a bit earthy, is too good for this writer to pass up.

It seems that just outside Wauchula, on the road over to Sebring, there is a retirement community that sports a nice semi-private 27 hole golf course. A fine clubhouse is located by a spacious parking lot, within easy reach by cart to the first tee starting hole of each nine. Of course the clubhouse has rest rooms, but there were none out on the course, and this set up a controversy that ensued among the male and female members of the links.

Some of the guys liked to have a few beers before they started their games, and a few would even stash a cold one in the coolers that they carried in their golf carts. Invariably, a foursome would be out on one of the holes a long way from the clubhouse, and a member would have to "make a visit." The most popular spot to stop was a thicket of trees that afforded good cover, the only drawback being that the winding golf cart path came around a corner there rather abruptly and some of the women came upon men zipping up or down when entering or leaving the forest.

So the women called a meeting to register a complaint with the guys, but since many of their husbands were in the men's league, may I say, word of their plans leaked out. By the time the good ole boys received an official protest, they called a gathering of their own and were ready for the ladies.

Their strategy was to take the offense, so they posted a notice on the main bulletin board declaring that in the interest of public relations and fair play among the two memberships of the course, they would not have any objections if the women wanted to use the same rustic glade as the males!

You can imagine the great excitement that this announcement caused in the ladies' locker room.

By coincidence, while all this was going on over a period of a few weeks, a horticultural team from the University of Florida, with permission from the course and the county, was checking out the woods in question and, lo and behold to their amazement and delight, came across a very, very rare type of orchid in the same ground that the men had fertilized.

The species in question, after much research, was found to be a Vanda brunner orchid, indigenous to Thailand, its natural habitat. (Tiger Woods' mother would surely know this.) Naturally, some of the boastful men were proud of this discovery and bragged that they had contributed to the growth and nurturing of the orchids over the years. Such pronouncements were seen as distasteful and drew icy stares from the women.

But yet, this turned out to be the right solution to the perplexing comfort station problem. The creative officers of the golf course held a Christmas orchid sale featuring the Vanda brunners, and people came from all over Florida to purchase them. The women golfers, good sports that they were, chipped right in and the affair turned a nice profit for the course. The money was used to erect a large wooden structure at the fringe of the orchid forest. In fact, it looked quite like the ice fishing shacks that you see every winter out on Lake Minnetonka, west of Minneapolis; edifices that also feature holes in the floor!

Chapter 19

Love Bugs And Golf

(Cousins to Maine's "No-See-Ums," You See Um Everywhere)

The poem below tells about Love Bugs and, as anyone that plays the game in the South will tell you, they are involved in the golfing picture twice a year for a week or so depending on the existing temperatures. They fly in tandem so you are facing two bugs at once, husband and wife. They will smear your clubs, your clothes, and your ball. Unlike the sneaky mosquito, they don't bite, but are terrible on navigation and seem to feature the head on collision, a la Warren Sapp of the football Tampa Bay Buccaneers, in their unplanned sacks. As the closing notice from the 'Save The Lovebug Society' reveals, they seem to have found a home in that quaint village of Wauchula, Fl.

LOVE BUG

Endemic to the Sunshine State
They appear in April and September,
Right about this time, every year
How do they remember?

Entwined, legs and lower body
One navigates the other attached.
Going where? end to end,
Wings aflapping, evenly matched.

Love bugs are not real swift
And stagger in their flight,
Circulating through the air
More in daytime than at night.

They shy away from the cold
And vanish in a freeze.
But with the temperature just right
You will find them on the breeze.

I spoke with a love bug yesterday.

Seemed a macho type to me,

Complaining that his wife was pregnant

So now he had to fly for three!

Tod McGinley

SAVE THE LOVEBUG SOCIETY
P.O. Box 2611
Sarasota, Florida 34230
(813) 957-0585
Zeta Hayes, President • *Bill Ayres, Vice-President*

March 4, 1995

Tod McGinley
Sun City Center, FL

INVITATION

You are cordially invited to be a part of the Dedication Ceremony April 1, and give your love bug poem.

Background: (See attached newspaper article)

At a December 15 Commission Meeting I proposed to the Hardee County Commissioners that the land surrounding the county courthouse in Wauchula be officially designated a love bug sanctuary.

To my great surprise — they agreed!

The Dedication Ceremony will be at 11 o'clock. Yes, Mr. McGinley, this will be Florida history in the making. Please do come — I need your support.

Sincerely,
Zeta Hayes

(Note the April Fool's date)

Chapter 20

Home Invasion Of The Maxflis

They are all gone away,
The house is shut and still
There is nothing more to say.
—Edwin Arlington Robinson

When my wife and I came to Florida several years back, we weren't quite clear on what an executive golf course was, as there were very few in Massachusetts, maybe one or two on Cape Cod. We now know that an executive course fits between a par three and a regulation layout, the difference being the yardage or length and size of the facility. Par for a regulation is usually 72 strokes, while an executive comes in between 55 to 65 swings.

And here is where some problems could surface. With homes often alongside a fairway, on an executive course out of bounds stakes are only 15 or 20 yards from structures, with balls striking roofs and windows, or landing in gardens. Folks that played the game before moving in recognize the potential for interesting things to occur, but the couple that is unfamiliar with the sport is not prepared for the subsequent golf ball invasion.

The following imagined conversation is more apt to take place under par three or executive course conditions. A golfer slices a ball out of bounds, into the garden of a non-playing new homeowner.

Homeowner: "Excuse me, sir, but what are you doing poking around in my hibiscus?"

Golfer (upset because he is out of bounds): "I'm looking for my golf ball. It's a new Maxfli."

Homeowner: "But the course is over there, why would your ball be in my flowers?"

Golfer: "Because I hit it here. I saw it land in here."

Homeowner (now perplexed): "You mean that you hit it here on purpose?"

Golfer: "No, no, it was not in my plans for the day."

Homeowner: "Well, please don't do it again!"

Golfer (now contrite): "OK, I'll try not to."

So, if you are looking for a home, and it is located on a golf course, be sure to inquire just "where" on the course. The 150-yard area from the tee box seems to be a logical place for golf ball invasion. The situation is rather like the people that move in close to an airport, and then wonder what the noise is all about!

Here are a few unique situations that have been reported over the past few years from retirement communities in various states.

• In Palm Springs, California— A man, tired of golfers in his back yard all day, staked a pit bull out there. Three months later he had a profit of more than $300 in selling experienced golf balls.

• In Naples, Florida— A woman controlled her sprinklers to soak invaders. She was a good sport about it and often invited neighbors over to watch and video this striking spectacle, where timing was everything!

• In Scottsdale, Arizona— A man got incensed when be spotted a golfer crushing his begonias under his spikes, while ball searching. Since he was a volunteer on security patrol, he put the unsuspecting golfer in a choke hold, cuffed him, read him his Miranda rights, and called the sheriff.

Perhaps Robert Frost knew a thing or two when he wrote "Good fences make good neighbors!

"In the alligator nation,
the word balata means bubble gum!"

Chapter 21

The Primal Scream

"And the loud laugh that spoke the vacant mind."
—The Deserted Village, William Goldsmith

Since we have mentioned putting quite often, it was in our plans to write a few lines about silence around the green, when there on my TV I came upon Tiger Woods and Billy Mayfair going head to head in the Nissan Open. They were on the verge of a playoff when Mayfair took the lead with a 5-foot putt. Tiger faced a 15 foot roll to the cup to force extra innings. Everyone surrounding the green was silent as Woods made the stroke, but when the ball was halfway to the cup, some boob screamed "IN THE HOLE" and to Tiger's disappointment, the ball slid past the cup.

Now, while it is true that the ball isn't affected by the scream, if you could see the glare that the player who misses under such circumstances sends toward the screamer, then you would know that such an outburst is most distracting to fans and players alike.

I am one who believes that the atmosphere around the fringe should be as hushed as the chapel in a Trappist monastery. This guy didn't even wait for the outcome of the putt, before he yelped. It reminds us of a scene that we are waiting to see happen someday on national TV during a football game.

A coach is standing there with his team ahead by one point and eight seconds left on the clock. It's December in Chicago and the temperature is 10°. Prematurely, several linemen (it's always linemen - backs don't do this) sneak up behind their unsuspecting mentor and dump a tub of greenish Gatorade over the poor man's head. At the same moment, on the field, his quarterback bobbles the snap up into the air, the opposition grabs the pigskin and runs it in for the winning score, leaving our man a soaking wet, freezing coach of the losing team!

But back to the golf green. It would be nice if in the future, when a screamer violates the sanctity of the area before a putt is finished, a nearby marshall would take him away, refund him his ticket price, and then give him a lifetime pass to all NASCAR racing events, where he can scream all he wants, and hopefully, forget the game of golf!

Chapter 22

The Paths Of Glory

He gave to Misery all he had, a tear;
He gained from (t'was all he wished),
a friend.

(Apologies to Thomas Gray)

When Thomas Gray wrote in his famous "Elegy In A Country Church-yard" that "the paths of glory lead but to the grave," we are quite sure that he wasn't referring to golf cart paths, although sometimes those little boulevards can contribute to disastrous situations. But Gray himself passed on in 1771 well before asphalt paths or golf carts. In fact, when he played, the ball was probably made of feathers so a birdie really was a birdie!

Starting with the premise that all devoted golfers will eventually find that great big bunker in the sky, it follows that some day in the future there will be cemeteries designed for deceased duffers only. People treat their pets that have left them, better than departed ballstrikers (re: Stephen King's "Pet Cemetery"). And it's not uncommon at all, these days to be playing a course and come upon a memorial marker over a club member's last remains.

At the popular Stow Acres course in Stow, Ma., there are two memorial plaques behind the bucolic 18th, par 5 finishing hole on the South course layout, a fitting location, it seems. They have been there for years, and the ashes of two players were scattered there. When I asked Tommy Page, one of the three Page brothers that started this 36-hole facility, if he planned for any more disposals, he replied, "Heck no, two's enough, we're not starting a cemetery here!" Present owner, Walter Lankau, has confirmed that the two original memorials can still be found behind the green. This is a long 530-yard, beautiful hole with a pond in the middle and a creek in front of the putting area. We wonder how a funeral procession would look, with musicians leading the way in the New Orleans manner, down the fairway from the tee to the green. Pretty impressive, we would think!

A cemetery for golfers? Perhaps there is one somewhere already. If not, it's just an idea before its time, but it probably will happen. There could be jobs created such as golf cemetery designers and Pete Dye* would be great at this! Last remains could be lowered into cups and flag sticks used as markers, one to 18 in a row. The paths could be named Driving Tee Lane, Bunker Avenue, Fairway Concourse or Duck Hook Highway. And it seems to us that the players that would really use such a facility, would be the high handicap golfer, the lifetime addict that meets the requirements of the Frostonian observation "they have nothing to look backward to with pride, and nothing to look forward to with hope." A cemetery for golfers would surely give them something to look forward to, a goal, so to speak.

And in such Elysium fields, a bad lie would be unthinkable!

(*Pete Dye is well known to most golfers. His reputation is as a golf course designer that creates most unusual and very difficult golf courses featuring island-type greens.)

A WHAT?!

Playing in Sun City Center awhile back at the tricky Challenger nine, part of the 27-hole Cypress Greens facility at Kings Point, we were in a foursome with some friends. The fifth hole there is a long 515-yard, par 5, with a pasture on the left, protected by a wire fence.

One of the guys was having real trouble from the tee. After he hit several out of bounds, it was suggested he take a Mulligan. When this went over a hill on the left, and we could not see if it went over or under the fence, there was silence. And then someone suggested a PROVISIONAL MULLIGAN! This must be a breakthrough in golf jargon, as none of us had ever heard this expression on the links before. (And it worked— he hit the next one smack down the middle!)

Chapter 23

A Nasty Little Hole

(Number 10 at Caloosa Greens, Sun City Center)

The hole pictured on the previous page is the 133-yard, par 3, number 10 at Caloosa Greens in Sun City Center, Fl. Look it over. Notice the large tree on the left that hangs out over the fairway and then the deep bunker to the right of the green. Adding to that is a fairway so narrow that, as Sam Snead once commented about another hole, "You have to walk single file to get to the flag."

That's not all. There's a five-foot drop behind the dance floor, and notice the foliage and bushes all along the right side. It's not visible, but housed inside that brush, is a 10-foot deep ravine with a stream running through it.

This little gem is one of the toughest and best-known holes here on the Gulf Coast of Florida. Yes, it's only a par three, but after I had tried to make my way through it a few times, I swore that I would gladly sign a legal document allowing me to pick up on the tee and take a four for the rest of my life.

Since this layout was only opened about five or six years ago, it is hard to dismiss the rumors that surround the 10th hole. Some members of the course insist that the verdant covering on the right contains the very stream John Huston used when he shot the classic picture, "The African Queen." They claim that this is the actual site where Humphrey Bogart was down in the water pulling Kate Hepburn along in the boat and he came out with leeches all over his body!

Here is a photo of two of my pals at the Caloosa Greens Golf Course. They are greens keeper Mike Smith and his capable assistant Johnnie O'Dell. I like them and they return the affection. They claim that after I finish 18 holes they pick up a lot of overtime repairing the facility! They also feel that they might lose me someday on the treacherous 10th hole where we believe that years ago the great movie director John Huston filmed his epic, "The African Queen."

Chapter 24

Give Up Golf! Who, me?

"For of all sad words of tongue or pen
the saddest are these:
It might have been!"

—Maud Muller
John Greenleaf Whittier

We were chatting with a fellow at the Florida Golf Writers meeting awhile back when he asked me a question that comes up with golfers every so often. "What would you be doing if you didn't spend so much of your time each week out on a golf course?" I am sure that a lot of men and women ball chasers ask themselves the same question, but it's one that I have never attempted to answer before, until that casual and unplanned inquiry.

The female golfers among our readers will tune in on my answer to the question regarding alternatives to golf quicker than the men. So please bear with me, as I explain why. Because of the Florida heat, most of the women are out on the courses in the morning. They routinely finish about lunch time and are home by noon. At 12:30 p.m., they turn on the TV to follow the romantic antics of a good looking rascal named Victor Newman. It seems that Mr. Newman is the main man on a soap called "The Young And The Restless."

Did I say that Victor was good looking? Let me put it this way, if Clark Gable ever came back to earth again, he would want to look like Victor Newman. In the show, Newman owns a company aptly named Newman Enterprises, and it doesn't take long to figure out just what his enterprises are all about.

So three times a week when I get back from the links, my wife, Carolee, who also is a golfer, will always have the show on as we sit down for a sandwich, and invariably, a beautiful woman will appear on the screen. "Who is that?" I will ask, and the answer is always the same, "Oh, she used to be married to Victor." It seems that our boy has been married and divorced at least seven or eight times, always to various fantastic lookers. I generally spend my lunch time staring at the screen, muttering comments like, "I can't believe this guy!" or just saying, a lot it seems, "Wow!" In fact, the only other male golfer that I know that watches the show, a friend named Jacques, got so upset when Victor left a stunning blonde named Ashley, that he refused to eat his lunch for three performances.

And that's what I would like to do if I had to make an exchange for a life without golf. With a little touch of the great tradition of "The Devil And Daniel Webster" or borrowing from the theme of "Damn Yankees" I would like to replace Victor Newman on "The Young And The Restless." I mean the man must be really worn out by now, anyway. The only thing that I might do a bit differently once I secured the position is, that instead of divorcing all these lovely women, I would move the show from L.A. or New York, to the outback of Utah, where such arrangements have not always been frowned upon, and spend the rest of my years walking around, smiling constantly, and devouring vitamins!

Some Quotes From Non-Pros

Whenever you go to a bookstore and find the golf section, you will surely notice the amount of humorous quotation works that have been assembled. The thing that gets my attention is that some of the best remarks are not from the professionals themselves, but rather from people who play the game and have gained their fame in some other field.

We have gathered together some of these observations and hope that the reader enjoys them as much as we do:

"I play in the low 50s. If it's any hotter than that, I won't play."
—Joe E. Lewis, nightclub entertainer
...

"I was three over— one over a house, one over a garage, and one over a swimming pool."
—George Brett, baseball great
...

"Your clubs."
—Jackie Gleason, TV star, when asked by club owner, Toots Shore, what to give his caddie after posting a high score
...

"The reason that the pro tells you to keep your head down, is so you won't see him bent over laughing."
—Phyllis Diller, TV star and comedienne
...

"I was on in nine strokes, had a 40-foot putt, and asked my caddie, 'How does this one break?' 'Who cares?' he said."
—Jack Lemmon, movie actor from Newton, Ma.
...

And finally, one of the greatest quotes that has endured for many years and is as strong as ever. It might be applied to golf, but, it's too pure to fool with, and is from an NFL coach. John McKay's Tampa Bay Buccaneers had just taken a terrible beating in an NFL contest, when he was asked, 'How do you feel about your club's execution?' He bluntly replied *"That's a good idea!"*

Chapter 25

An Indoor Winter Putting Drill

(Designed especially for our northern golfing friends in Minnesota and Massachusetts)

We were talking long distance to our son, Joe, up in Massachusetts last winter, and he was lamenting the fact that he had a few feet of snow out in his yard in Norton and was not able to get out there to swing a club. After inviting him and his wife, Sue, down to Florida I tried to console him with instructions for a new indoor putting drill that I had just worked into my own pregame practice routine.

The procedure had been triggered after we had observed on national TV, late one Sunday afternoon, an incident that shocked thousands of viewers. In fact, on Monday morning it was all that the golfers could talk about in our local clubhouse. In a large tournament, the leader missed a 2-foot putt! Now, as a writer that broke in covering high school football and could not bring himself to reporting the name of the halfback that fumbled away the pigskin because his mom and dad felt bad enough without reading about it the next day, I won't identify the PGA player. It doesn't matter now and he did go on to win the match. But it really got me thinking about how, too often, the average golfer does not show respect for the short putt, let alone practice it.

In football when an announcer says that a team is in short yardage position, it sends a tremor of excitement out to the audience, because it means that something interesting is likely to occur on the next play. So we are taking advantage of that built-in conditioning among golfing sports fans, and calling any 3-foot (a yard) putt, a short yardage situation.

Now here are the simple steps to set up the drill. All that is required is a putter and two golf balls. Pick a spot on your living or family room carpet, and put one ball down. Behind it three feet away, place the second or rear ball. Assume your putting posture and stroke one ball into the back of the other, like a billiard shot. What you will discover after a few efforts is that when hit 100 percent perfect, the forward ball will carry straight ahead about seven inches or so, without bend or deviation. If your attempt is off just the slightest, the front ball will veer to the right or left.

That's it. This is the short yardage putting drill to employ next winter when you are stranded in the house during a blizzard. It doesn't cost a dime and you won't need any more equipment than what you already have in your bag. Yes, we are aware that this will cut down on the popular "gimmee" often employed in casual rounds in order to speed up play. And you probably won't hear any more shouts of I.G.A (inside the give area) or O.G.A (outside the give area), when you are out there by the greens.

The indoor short yardage exercise is always run on a nice, flat carpet or rug layout. We are aware that aeration punctures, inclines and declines and little dips won't be found in your living room, and there's nothing harder than a three foot downhill putt that has to break right. Probably St. Anthony has to find a way out of those situations for you!

One closing observation about our indoor drill. If you practice it and gain proficiency in getting one ball to "kiss" another, you will surely gain more accuracy than you would if you were using the wider indoor cups that are on the market. And again... you can't beat the price!

In our Florida community there are six very popular golf courses. So it was no surprise when at a crowded Sunday Mass an usher walked to our pew, called out "four" signifying empty spaces — and everybody ducked!

—*Tod McGinley*

As printed in the Catholic Digest, October 1997.

Now That's Real Focus

Two golfers are on the 18th green in a close contest for more than a few bucks. One guy has an eight-foot putt to win the match. He's set over the ball, when the other golfer speaks up, "Hey, Al, I saw your wife leaving a motel this morning with —."

The guy over the putt interrupts him, "Hold that thought a second LeRoy, I want to concentrate on this one."

Unexpected Gust

The well known singing golfer, Don Cherry, veteran of Masters and Ryder Cup play, entertained his Florida audiences recently with this story:

It seems that a golfer down in Wichita Falls, Texas, who had difficulty all his life with keeping his drive in the fairway, passed away. His will requested that his golfing buddies rent a helicopter and release his ashes over his favorite hole on the course. They did this and when they were up in the air right over the center of the fairway, they poured the contents of the urn out through the hatch of the copter — only to watch helplessly as a sudden breeze carried the remains out of bounds!

Chapter 26

The Athlete

(The guy was a natural)

A while back, when some of my golfing pals were out of town and I was looking for a game, I called the local clubhouse and was told to "come on over, we'll get you out with somebody".

When I arrived, the starter introduced me to Charley, who was down from Detroit, Michigan, looking over our golfing community as a possible retirement site. As we chatted on the putting green awaiting our tee time, I asked him how he liked out little town. "Well," he replied "since I consider myself a jock, I think it's just terrific. There's so much to do here for an athletic person like myself." He then went on to say that he was a good swimmer and diver, and, excelled at softball, tennis and basketball!

Wow, I thought, what did the starter do to me, fixing me, an 18 handicapper, up with someone like this? As we got up by the first tee I was impressed by his practice swings, nice and easy, good tempo with a nice turn and excellent follow through on the ball. The first hole is a basic 375 yards, not very difficult, par four. Charley shot an eight! Oh, well, I thought, maybe he's a little tired from the trip down from the north, and besides, it didn't seem to bother him a bit. A likable fellow, he kept laughing and smiling.

The second hole on our course is a 450 yard par 5, and after losing two balls, Charley managed to get down in 10 strokes. And so it went, he was all over the place. Since we were using my cart, I thought of charging him mileage. I saw places on that course that I didn't even know were there. He was in the woods, on people's lawns, and several times drove sunning alligators back into their ponds. The funny thing is that he kept making remarks such as "I really belted that one," or "Watch me nail this sucker."

Sometimes when we were on the green, he would smile at me and comment "never up, never in" and then proceed to stroke the ball 12 feet past the cup! Charley was something else. After about six or seven holes I started trying to think of an excuse that I could use in order to avoid going on to the second nine. I finally came up with my old stand-by, that my "golf elbow" was starting to bother me in my back swing. He was very gracious about that.

I tried to get away without commenting on his game. I lost count but my estimate is that he shot about a 68 on the first nine while losing about seven balls. Charley did say that he felt that he "was a little off today." I'll say he was off — off the fairway and off the course. Trying to think of a response to that, I mentioned that maybe he would get more involved down here with some of the other sports that he had mentioned, softball or tennis. He just beamed at me and said, "NO WAY. GOLF IS MY BEST GAME!"

*   *   *

(A WORD OF CAUTION-

Whenever you get into a golf match with a stranger, it's a good idea not to wager with the fellow, if he is wearing a handcuff key around his neck!)

Chapter 27

The Seeing Eye Dog Putter

(It does everything but lick your face)

First off, we should explain that we have never heard of a club named The Seeing Eye Dog Putter. Since we have owned many putters and know the names of most of the ones that are on the market, we feel that we are on safe ground with this label. Also, we are happy if, in some way, we are inventing this title, because that means that no one else can use it, maybe.

I thought of the name because I have become aware of the terrific sales pitches on golf equipment that have been coming at us from TV lately, and a lot of them are aimed at selling putters. We saw one this past week that was on for about half an hour, and was hard hitting and repetitive.

With our Seeing Eye Dog Putter, we would get the ad writers to stress that besides being a deadly ball guide to the hole, the putter would feel warm to the touch, be loyal, faithful and friendly, just like a dog, and do everything but lick your face. Teaching pros from all over the country would appear on our TV ad and practically guarantee the golfer that they could hole those 25 foot breaking putts that have always evaded them.

Of course, the close TV shots would be edited and most selective. The viewer at home is only shown the putts that drop into the cup, and these are putted by professionals on manicured surfaces, under perfect conditions. The panel of pro models, laughing and smiling, display disbelief as putt after putt from the Seeing Eye Dog Putter finds the hole on every stroke!

The Seeing Eye Dog Putter would be sold by one of the best methods ever invented, Dale Carnegie's basic principles of selling — Attention, Interest, Conviction, Desire and Close. I ran a pilot film of our Seeing Eye Dog Putter sales presentation and put myself through the Carnegie test. Here are the results.

ATTENTION ... Did the sales pro get my attention? Yes, of course he did. I play golf at least three times a week and am a terrible putter, but I love dogs— once had a great, black lab named Ike.

INTEREST ... Did the pitch get my attention? Yes, I stopped eating to eye the kitchen TV, pushed my filet mignon to the side and never finished it.

CONVICTION... Was I convinced that The Seeing Eye Dog Putter was as good as they said? I think so. I started calling the 800 number before the ad was over. All the lines were busy. Next case.

DESIRE ... Was a desire for the putter created? By all means, since I couldn't get through on the phone, I took a cab to the Tampa airport and flew out to the Seeing Eye Dog Putter factory located in La Mirada near Los Angeles, all on the same day!

CLOSE... Was the sale closed? Yes, when I put it on my MasterCard that I would pay $100 a month for the easy payment method of three months, I closed the sale myself.

We checked with the sales department of The Seeing Eye Dog Putter company later on to find out how sales were going. They told us that shipments around the country were very, very heavy.

At a recent sales meeting it was reported that the TV ad promotion was so persuasive, that The Seeing Eye Dog Putter people heard from many prospects that normally would not be considered as potential customers for a golf club. Here's a few of them:

- Three inmates, with no chance of pardon or parole, on the death row cell block at Huntsville State Prison in Texas, ordered one Seeing Eye Dog Putter apiece.

- Two U.S. Navy submariners in New London, Connecticut, saw the commercial on a TV set over a bar and were so influenced that they dashed into an adjoining golf store and purchased two putters. They didn't even think of golf balls as they immediately boarded a nuclear sub to go on a cruise underneath the Arctic Circle ice cap.

- In Aberdeen, South Dakota, a 92-year-old man who has been a resident of a rest home for five years and never leaves the building, let alone goes golfing, after watching the commercial for The Seeing Eye Dog Putter, picked up a phone and was ordering two of them, before a curious nurse intervened.

Was the TV blitz a success? You bet, and be sure to watch for the new one, when we commence promoting our latest product — a $1,000 driver featuring a rubber head on an elastic shaft, that will drive your tee shot 500 yards! We guarantee it. It's going to be called The Bungee Jumper Driver!

Chapter 27

A Final Word

(Work at finding ways to enjoy golf more, look around, it will astound you)

In Florida, once in awhile we hit a high shot with a number five or a seven wood up into a blue sky with white clouds sailing underneath and we hardly watch the ball landing as the scene above is so mesmerizing. We like to call this the wonderment of golf. It reminds us of the journey that the bird takes in Johnny Mercer's song "Skylark" where he cites some picturesque spots and then requests "but my heart is riding on your wings, so if you see them anywhere won't you leave me there." This great game holds wonderment and also curiosity for the participant. How many times have you come upon the tee box on a course that you are playing for the first time, and without looking at the yardage on the card, exclaim to your partners, "Wow, this hole must be 600 yards long" only to find that it's really 420 yards? And then after you bop a drive out there about 200 yards and you arrive at the ball, you get a totally different look from what you thought you viewed from the tee.

There can be a lot of fun garnered from a round of golf. The game finds room for everyone and we should accept what the course gives us on any particular day. I have found that the real trick for me is to put two good nines together, but it should not be a case of life or death out there.

In our travels we have been fortunate enough to have played all over the country, plus Canada, Puerto Rico, and St. Thomas, and, I have never met a course that I didn't like. In fact, I can't recall meeting many golfers that I didn't like. A president of Boston University once said of the human condition, "We are a dime a dozen — and we are magnificent!" He could have been talking about golfers.

So, fellow golfers, keep swinging, and as I wrote at the start of this book, surely every once in awhile you will strike a ball just as good as Jack or Arnie, or Jane Geddes ever hit. And the memory of that shot will keep coming back like a song, a song that keeps saying 'remember!'. Friends, that's what this game is all about!

A Golfer's Thank You Note
To God

Thank you very, very much
    for this truly wonderful game,
Where every hole is a thrilling journey
    And they're never quite the same.

Thanks for the green, green grass
    And all the beautiful trees,
That can be seen on every fairway
    As we gaze out from the tees.

Also thanks for blue, blue skies
    And even the wandering streams,
That catch our slicing shots and
    Interrupt our most ardent dreams.

And thanks for truly great friends
    We have played with over the years,
Who have shared our greatest joys
    And understood our occasional tears.

And one final remark, dear God,
    About this game that's so much fun,
Do you think you could possibly arrange
    For me to make a hole-in-one?

An Invitation

A newspaper that we write golf articles for is named the Sun City Center Observer News. It is located in Ruskin, Florida, and is delivered to about 20,000 homes in southern Hillsborough County. Sometimes the name of the paper is different in each community, but I prefer the name Observer. I have seen it called The Shopper, but that reminds me too much of Annie Proulx's popular 1994 best seller "The Shipping News" which is about a paper in a Newfoundland fishing village. Somehow when a paper that I write for is called The Shopper, I have a feeling that it is going to end up wrapping fish, and that some haddock will be closer to my essay than any reader.

Anyway, once in a great while, we receive an inquiry about golf that comes to us through the Observer office. If they are signed we will attempt to handle them, sometimes consulting a local pro. One note came to us awhile back but was only signed "Embarrassed" so I assume that the writer hoped that we would answer them in a future column.

It seems that this person took lessons from a pro up in the Boston area last summer and later got mixed up in the instructions. They were told that they would be let in on one of golf's great "secrets." A move that would add 15 or 20 yards to their drives! The secret advice was that when they were getting ready to play golf, they should tie one shoelace tight and one shoelace loose. It had something to do with making the weight transfer go smoother but our letter writer came home to Florida and got confused on which foot should be tied tightly and which foot should be tied loosely. Could we help him out?

Frankly, dear reader, we had never heard of such a "golf secret" like this before, and since the story came out of New England, I considered writing to one of my favorite golf authors, John Updike, who plays the game up on the North Shore outside Boston, and whose recent book "Golf Dreams" shows that he would have the capability to solve this problem. But a better solution occurred to us that could be some fun and do a lot of good where it's needed.

We would consult some local pros in Florida, as there are many fine instructors here on the West Coast, as well as the excellent teaching pros at the local Don Sutton Golf School in Sun City Center, a nationally known campus. Then we would print instructions of their interpretation of the shoe lace "golf secret."

We now are asking you, our readers, to send to us any ideas you may have on solving the problem along with a donation to our refuge for abused women and their children. When you receive our thank you note, along with it you will receive our written consolidated opinion, that should bring closure to this irksome shoelace dichotomy. Is it a deal? If so, please send your solution along with a donation to:

Mary & Martha House, Inc.
P.O. Box 1251
Ruskin, FL 33570-1251

Thank you, I look forward to hearing from you!

Appendix

As I Recall

My introduction to golf was in a dusty, old ball field outside Keene, New Hampshire, in a very hot July many years ago. My father, Mac, had just taken up the game and he would place brother, Joe and me, out in the field with our baseball gloves, and then commence to hit golf balls to us. Though Mac was a good athlete, he was a novice to golf and his shots were all over the place. After about an hour under the sun, Joe and I would be running around out there with our tongues hanging out, pleading to go back to our rented cottage by Lake Conticook.

Mac stayed with the game, improved, and the next summer we found ourselves down near Cape Cod. Our cousins, Joe and Bud Harris, were at a Cape caddie camp near Woods Hole, so they saw that we got plenty of old clubs and balls. Back then you could play all day on a course after you paid the green fee of $2 or so. Dad would drop brother Joe and me off in the morning on a little 9-hole layout outside Wareham, and come back for us, late in the afternoon. We happily would start out playing together, but when Mac came back for us six or seven hours later, he would find me on one hole and Joe on another. What usually happened was that Joe would lose a ball in the rough, and I would start looking for it with him. I would sometimes find a ball or two, but neither one would be Joe's. After this happened a few times he would become angry with me, stalk off and play by himself! He claimed that I wasn't really looking for his ball, but was taking advantage of the situation to add to my own supply! I can still see Joe off there on a fairway three or four holes away from me. When Mac came back to get us, he would have to walk out on the course, and round us up — he got a big kick out of that. After a while, as we grew older, it would be a treat for us, and later my younger brother, Paul, to join Mac or my uncles Herman Evers or Frank Harris for a round.

When we hit high school, we got quite involved in baseball, football and hockey, but also felt that the 10 or 12 times that we got out on a course during summer, qualified us to call ourselves "golfers." We also caddied on occasion. North of Boston, Mac would take us to a nine hole facility in Lynnfield Center, and when we were ready for an 18 hole track, we moved over to Sagamore in Lynnfield, Colonial in Wakefield and Unicorn in Stoneham.

Who are those guys? Vern Mikkelsen, left, and Jim Holstein, far right, were teammates on the championship Minneapolis Lakers team. We got together at the Tara Country Club in Bradenton, Florida, just before Mik was inducted into the NBA Hall of Fame in Springfield, Massachusetts. Jim coached basketball at Ball State in Muncie, Indiana, before coming to Florida. He is an excellent golfer.

Minnesota Days

In the early 1950s we left a daytime selling job and night work in the sports department of the Boston Herald to stop by New York briefly and then took a sales position in Minnesota.

By last count I have played golf in 27 states, two provinces, Puerto Rico and St. Thomas. I tried Cyprus once when visiting daughter-in-law Toula's family, but the game wasn't established on that beautiful island yet. The majority of my golf has been played in Massachusetts and Minnesota. As a young salesman we were on the road quite a bit and always had the clubs in the trunk. I was very fortunate in that I was employed by "one of the best 100 companies to work for in the United States," the H.B. Fuller Co. of St.

Paul, Minnesota. Of course as the game grew, and popular President Dwight Eisenhower had some effect here, golf was a nice way to spend time with customers, and then sales meetings started allowing time on the links, to be put on the agenda.

Over the years we were involved in some leagues and various tournaments. A few other people and I started a nice little 9-hole event in late afternoon after work at H.B. Fuller. We played the Como course in St. Paul and had loyal attendance from the lab, production, sales and headquarters staff. It was great fun and I recall, playing at various times with Pete Flock, Dick Koch, Russ Kopp, Dick Steinke, Jim Dougherty, Ed Murphy, Ralph Reichow, "Father" Jerry Blees, Len Humphrey, Dick Johnson, Curt Feyen, Tony Andersen, Chuck Brauer, Jim Watt, John Ray, Dave Swanson and Jerry McGinty. When people from around the country would visit the main office they would come out to Como I remember Les Brenno, Keith Smith, Kermit Jorgensen, Dick Schnittker. The treasurer, Dave Croonquist, was an excellent golfer; Jerry Slavin, Al Vigard, Jim Collins, Frank Beutel, Frank Durham, Bill Dunn, Harvey Goesch, Ed Davis, Dick McGowan, Ward Oliver, Dick E. Smith, Bob Odom, Bob Broos, Bob Brown, Dave McKnight, Rolf Schubert, Ward Oliver, Wally Ostlie, Dale Pierson, Bruce Sanson, Al Fischer, Bernie Juba, Darrell Babcock, Walt Meyer, John Fisher, Fred Dinger, Dick W. Smith, Bill Stone, Orion Felland, Bill Testor, Joe Hall, Don Wiskow, Curt Held, Dean LaVelle, George McDougall, Rod McEwen, Rich Weeks, Frank Hixon and Arvid Johnson

Around the country, over the years we have played at various meetings in Georgia, Florida and Kentucky with Don Rigot, Gene Hollo, Steve Salvato, Ed B. Davis, Doug Deitz, Dick Knight, Gerry Scott, Steve Tary, Billy Dunn, Don Debord, Jack Gerling, Jim Kadidlo, Vic Vitelli, Jack Pennington, Bill Rumohr, John Rodeck, Bill Smith, Doug Kaiser, Rich Mongeau, Elliot Tuqua and Dave Goetz.

There were many fine courses around the Twin Cities. The city of Minneapolis itself ran five or six very good ones. We recall playing at

Meadowbrook, Hiawatha, Gross, Columbia and Wirth. At one time I lived with several Laker basketball players and two other friends, Mark Schulstad and John Roberts. We played Wirth with Hall of Famer Vern Mikkelsen, Jim Holstein (former Ball State coach) and Lew Hitch. Years later at Wirth I was with brother-in-law Jack Nagel and my wife's uncles, Ray and Vince Meyers, when Vince got an ace on a 160-yard hole.

Over at Meadowbrook we used to go out with Harold Lindberg, Rich Mongeau, Roger Grant, John Roberts, Dick Schnittker and Jack Moroni. After our marriage I got Carolee playing a bit, and later we started taking the boys, Joe, Dan and Steve, to the driving range at Braemer in Edina. We had moved over from south Minneapolis and built a house in Edina, and the town had great recreational facilities. There are 36 holes at Braemer, a par 3, a monster driving range, archery section and two indoor hockey rinks, plus a large indoor golfing building for winter practice. Carolee and I would play with close friends, Gene and Arla Olive, and Don and Gene Rogers. I also played there with friend, Jack Patera, who was a Vikings coach at the time and later was the initial coach of the Seattle Seahawks.

There were some fine tournaments around the Twin Cities in those days, and I remember Billy Martin, then a coach with the Twins, as well as Jim Finks and Jerry Reichow, of the Vikings, taking part in popular restaurant owner Joe Duffy's affair.

Minnesota All-American football player and good friend Bob McNamara who played in the Canadian League with Winnipeg, and with the Denver Broncos, had a tournament out of his restaurant lounge over near the University campus. We emceed at the awards affair afterwards and a host of Vikings football players took part. They were Bill "Boom-Boom" Brown, Chuck Lamson, Tommy Franckhauser, Dean Derby, among Viking players, Ed Sharockman, Jerry Reichow, Roy Winston, as well as guest Paul McGuire, who is now a very successful NFL announcer. We played in those days often with a good golfer and Viking quarterback, John McCormick, who had been a star at UMass. John is the only witness to the one time in my life that I broke 80. I shot a 39-40 at the short, but regulation course, Columbia, in Northeast Minneapolis, one spring day. John and his lovely wife, Gail, reside in Golden, Colorado, since he retired from the Denver club and we still keep in touch.

Packerland

In my travels for H.B. Fuller, it came about that we visited Green Bay, Wisconsin and the Fox River Valley area quite a bit. Over the years we played golf at Brown County course, Fox River, Butte des Morts and Oneida Hunt Club links.

At Oneida I remember playing with Dick Schnittker in front of a foursome that included Bart Starr and Coach Vince Lombardi of the Green Bay Packers. Afterwards in the locker room I visited with Vince about mutual friends that we had up in Boston, folks that he had met as a coach and recruiter when he was on the West Point staff. But what I most recall about him was his repeating, several times, that "This game of golf is going to make me a basket case!"

We combined golf with some business and had a sports dinner in Green Bay where we flew over friends Mick Tingelhoff and Bill Brown of the Minnesota Vikings, and they joined Boyd Dowler and Big Mike McCoy of the Packers. Tony Andersen, then President of Fuller, and current board chair, helped us run the appreciation evening for our many customers, and it was great fun.

Later, we played down in Butte Des Morts Golf Club in Appleton, Wisconsin, in the 1,000 Yard Golf Classic. This event was a charitable affair that benefited the youth of Wisconsin. It was put together by Fred "Fuzzy" Thurston of the Packers, and it was my privilege to be emcee at a lively golf dinner that included such notables as Max McGee, Jim Taylor and Paul Hornung of the Packers, as well as Pittsburgh Steelers' John Henry Johnson, Denver's Floyd Little, and the Cleveland Browns' LeRoy Kelly. These were all great football players, but that day they were just a bunch of guys trying to hit a golf ball! H.B. Fuller representatives, Pete Flock, Joe Orheck, Ed Degenhardt and Dick Schnittker, did a super job for our company in this very nice part of Wisconsin.

The author, Tod McGinley (on right end in photo), was in Appleton, Wisconsin to emcee the dinner after golf at Fuzzy Thurston's 1,000 Yard Classic. It was a celebrity affair but a fullback from the Chicago Bears couldn't get up there. When Tod asked Fuzzy who the celebrity was in his foursome, he was told, "I guess you are!"

Back To Mass

When we write "Back to Mass" we are not talking about going to church, but rather, our family's move from Minnesota, where Carolee was born, to Massachusetts, my birthplace (Malden). The H.B. Fuller Co. asked us to manage their New England operation, and we agreed to, but it was awful tough to leave the old Gopher state. Minnesota gave me my wife, Carolee, and three great sons, Joe, Dan and Steve, all born in Minneapolis.

But New England has been good also and the boys finished their educations there at Amherst College, University of Rhode Island, and UMass. They also met three wonderful girls who became McGinleys. So it's Sue and Joe, Jane and Dan, and Toula and Steve.

Sue and Jane are Bay Staters, and, Toula is a proud native of Cyprus. So far, for grandchildren, we have Meghan and Lee and Andreas and Jonathan.

In Mass we settled in the bucolic village of Sudbury, located about 30 miles northwest of Boston, a town with the historic zip code of 01776! The boys all played the usual sports of football, baseball and hockey, but with an acre and a half of land, we got them swinging a few golf clubs. They had been to the range and par-three in Edina, Minnesota, so they weren't totally unfamiliar with the game. Today they all play with me and Carolee whenever we get together at Cape Cod or here in Florida.

Fortunately, Sudbury is located among some fine golf facilities. Nearby is Stow Acres, a 36-hole course that has hosted the U.S. Amateur. Butternut, also is in the town of Stow, and Wayland is the home of the Wayland Country Club and Sandy Burr. To the west is the Marlboro Country Club, where I was first invited to by cousin Leo Evers, and, it was the site of Senior PGA matches for years. A member and close friend, John Murray, who has a keen interest in our "Ambrose Mulligan" story, had us over there so often that he referred to me as "America's Greatest Guest." H.B. Fuller supported the chamber of commerce outings at Marlboro every year, and we also had our own little event, The Fuller Open, at Juniper Hills in neighboring Northborough.

Two of our salesmen were very good golfers, Ed Barry and Ron Lufkin. Ed was a member of the prestigious Tedesco course up in the North Shore town of Marblehead. Ron and I entertained customers often out on Worcester and Springfield links. Another great layout near Sudbury, is Nashawtuc Country Club on the Concord-Sudbury boundary. Ed Thompson, a town administrator, who also has more than a passing interest in the ongoing saga of "Ambrose Mulligan," often joined me there as we were guests of a prominent Boston barrister, Tom Dignan.

The Hartigan Memorial is held every year at the Wayland Country Club, and John Treacy and Dan McCarthy and I were among the original founding fathers. It is named after Father Jack Hartigan, a wonderful pastor of Our Lady of Fatima Church, who was also a state police chaplain, WWII Pacific veteran, and avid golfer. He shot three aces in his career. After he passed on, the tournament was named in his honor, and the Rev. Stan Russell, a Congregational minister, was one of our biggest supporters. Stan loved to golf, and his eventual demise took two great churchmen from Sudbury.

Before Fr. Hartigan's death, the affair was called Our Lady of Fatima Open. Carolee and Jeanne McCarthy, Dan's wife, and some other women would serve pizzas in the church basement after the golf. The golfers in the parish were lucky when it was found out that the new pastor, Fr. Foley from Beverly, Massachusetts, also loved the game. The tournament was then held at the Wayland Country Club and about 50 people, men and women, would take part.

That called for a nice gathering after the match and an awards dinner run by John Treacy. Among contestants over the years, we recall Dr. Maurice Fitzgerald, Ed Thompson and Jack Murray of the Mulligan connection; Tom Dignan, Joe McGinley, Ron Lufkin, Al La Freniere, Dan McCarthy, Jack McCarthy, John Treacy (John's wife, Terry, and his sisters helped with the registrations); Dr. Tom Gelsinon and son, Brendan; Bob Hurstak, Frank Vana, Tom Welch, Fran Kearns, Bill Thompson, Dick Andrews, Fred Vorderer, John Lanigan, John Pellegri, Dave Harvey, Steve Blanchette, Tony Scafidi, Dick Babineau and quite a few other Sudbury folks.

Over at Juniper Hills in Northboro, Ron Lufkin and Bobby Drake gathered some employees together each summer for the H.B. Fuller affair and dinner. Ed Barry, Jim Hayden, Glenn Mac Donald, Mike Gilbert, Dale Pierson, Tom McAndrews, Dave Quail, Tim Schmitt, Nick DeRose, Paul Lazazzero, Billy Cox and invited guests Dan McCarthy, Al Le Freniere and Steve McGinley sometimes joined us. The office staff would attend the dinner and it was nice to have Jean Petrosky, Bonny Clark, Carolyn Parenti and Angela Addeo to share in the good humor that prevailed.

As the years with H.B. Fuller went by, we piled up more vacation time, and a lot of it was used for golf. Either in business or pleasure, we played many New England and a few New York courses. Bob Shannon would have Ed Barry and me over to Bear Hill in Stoneham yearly, and Ed and I played every summer with a customer named Bill Staples, up at Aroostook Valley, in Ft. Fairfield, Maine. Most of the course is close to the St. John River in Canada, and it is one of the most scenic layouts that we have ever gone out on. My dad, Mac, was born in that area of New Brunswick. The clubhouse is situated in Maine, so its truly an international game there.

Of course now that we reside in Florida, we only play in New England two or three times a summer. This is usually at one of the beautiful Cape Cod clubs, The Captains, Cranberry Valley, or New Seabury. But during our last trip, a good friend, Larry La Freniere invited his uncle Al and me, and Joe Sullivan, to play Pleasant Valley in Sutton, Massachusetts. This is an excellent challenge that has been a PGA stop for years. Maybe Jack Murray is correct, there might be something to the label "America's Greatest Guest" that he hung on yours truly!

The old McGinley line — My brother Paul on the left, and Joe on the right are about to destroy the myth that good hockey players make good golfers. The event was the annual McGinley Open held at the Wampanoag Country Club in West Hartford, Connecticut. The title is currently occupied by Beasley Reece, a nine-year NFL veteran and CBS football announcer.

The McGinley Open

In Meriden, Connecticut, on June 20, 1975 a terrible accident occurred that took the life of 14-year-old Brian McGinley. The young boy, son of Pat and Paul McGinley, was walking down a street when he was struck from behind by an automobile driven by two teenagers. All the McGinleys and relatives and their friends were devastated, when this beautiful lad was taken from us.

Out of this tragedy, the family gathered closer, and every year after that, wonderful sister-in-law Pat, and my brother Paul held a McGinley picnic in Meriden. A lot of the nephews and our sons were taking up golf then, so it was natural that a McGinley Open was put together by Brian's brothers, Mark and Robby.

For more than 20 years this event (although not sanctioned by the PGA!) has been held at Bayberry Hill on the Cape and in Connecticut at Lyman Orchards, Hunters Green, and more recently at Wampanoag in West Hartford. My brother Paul and sons, Mark and Bob, and his son-in-law, Rick Paisker, play every year. Brother Joe comes over from New Jersey, with wife, Martha, and sons John and Phil, to participate. Our boys Joe, Danny and Steve have also joined the field. Fr. Mark Jette of Meriden is a golfer and also our chaplain. (He carries a clergical dispensation that allows him a Mulligan on the first tee!)

Of the guests and celebrities that have been attracted to this tournament, the most outstanding scores have been turned in by a former NFL defensive back and end, Beasley Reece. This gentleman spent nine years in pro football with the Dallas Cowboys, Tampa Bay Buccaneers, and New York Giants. He was a hitter on the football field and is a hitter on the golf course; he can really smack a ball. Beasley has his own sports TV show in Philadelphia and will be on NFL telecasts for CBS Sundays this fall. We wish him well. He has secured an exemption to play in the McGinley Open for years to come!

Out of fairness to the various courses in New England that compete to hold this tournament each year, co-chairmen Mark and Bob, have decided to spread it around. In this summer of 1998 the gathering of the clan will return to Cape Cod in July.

Many of the clubs seen at the McGinley affair are produced by cousin Joe Harris of St. Joseph, Missouri. We visited St. Joe several years ago, and while Carolee went shopping with Rosemary Harris, Joe and I and Kansas City friend John Roberts played the local country club. Joe is a Class A member of the Professional Clubmakers Society and has been making custom made products for local pros and amateurs, in the area for years. It was great fun soaking up the golfing atmosphere of his busy shop for a few days and testing clubs on Joe's backyard range.

At Last, Florida

I guess that it's something that a lot of golfers, men and women, probably have in the back roads of their minds for years: retiring from the job up in Minnesota or Michigan, Maine or Massachusetts, and moving down to Florida where they can swing the club year round. The first time we came to Florida was back in 1948 to see a high school football game in Jacksonville, where Malden High defeated Lee High, in a post season game at the Gator bowl. Didn't even bring my golf clubs!

Years later there were business meetings, with an afternoon for golf, held at great spots like Doral in Miami, the Bonadventure in Fort Lauderdale and Mission Inn at Howey-In-The-Hills, northwest of Orlando. Being at those places was enough for me. Though I still had some years before retirement, the seed was planted.

If you are reading these words and are still working, you will hear that Florida is filling up. Don't be concerned. Although the big cities on each coast are crowded, and especially the Orlando area in the center of the state, there is still tons of room down here for development. Take a look at a map, and locate Sun City Center, south of Tampa about 20 miles by I-75. Every winter my brother Joe and our friend Bob Shannon get together over in Vero Beach. We always pick a golf course somewhere between Sun City Center and Vero where we can meet and play. Generally, it's at a nice layout on Route 60 called Indian Lake Estates. This past year my brother Paul joined me and we started east from Sun City Center on State Road 674. We drove through hamlets like Fort Lonesome, Fort Meade, and Frostproof and up through Lake Wales. Paul, who is from Meriden, Connecticut, near Hartford, was amazed at the space out there. For long periods, we were the only automobile on the road!

Sun City Center itself is one of the premier golfing retirement communities in the country. Among some 14,000 residents are 126 holes on six courses, plus four driving ranges and practice areas, and construction of another course is under way! And if you ever want to get "off campus" for a change, and we all do this, there are three excellent public courses within 15 minutes. Right next door in Ruskin is Cypress Creek, a great facility, while over at Apollo Beach by the bay, is the Robert Trent Jones designed Golf and Sea Club. Just seven short miles up U.S. 301, nationally know amateur, Beth Bauer, plays and practices at the fine Summerfield Crossings Golf Club. As many of our Canadian friends have observed "It's a golfer's hat trick." Also, people from all over Canada and the U.S. register yearly at the outstanding Ben Sutton Golf School here in Sun City Center.

To paraphrase a great movie line from "Field of Dreams," a golfer might arrive down here and inquire, "Am I in heaven?" to which we would reply, "No, it's just Florida!"

"We golfed in the sunshine, we laughed every day, and I went on my way, and I went on my way."

And to conclude this proposition, it seems that some pretty fair golfers named Nicklaus, Palmer and Snead might agree, after all, they moved to the Sunshine State a long time before Tiger Woods and I got here!!

Thanks and Acknowledgments

It's funny the different ways that people get started writing. About 1941 at Malden Catholic High School in Malden, Massachusetts, where I was a freshman, the hockey coach, Bro. Armand C.F.X., made a deal with me. He would allow me to be a playing-manager on the varsity team, and whenever M.C. got a few goals in front in a contest, he would put me out there for a shift or two. My end of the deal was that after the game I would run the write-ups of the event, up to the *Malden Evening News* in Malden Square. After awhile, I was writing the few lines that went with the statistics myself. So thank you, Bro. Armand.

As we continued early editors were Harold Harding and Tom Kenny at *The News,* and frien, Gerry Weidmann of the school paper, who later had a successful career as an editor at the *Boston Globe*. We became a stringer for the *Boston Post* and the *Globe,* covering high school football and hockey, and later combined a daytime selling job with night work at the then *Boston Herald Traveler* under Ralph Wheeler.

With "Mulligan's Name Was Ambrose," there are many people that lent help, interest and assistance. Wife Carolee, as secretary and booking agent, former *Boston Globe* editor and later of the *Framingham News* and the *Boston Tab*; Bob Moore, who scanned early articles at Marrone's Bake Shop in Sudbury, Massachusetts; and Marguerite and Al La Freniere of Acton, Massachusetts, both critics, friends and supporters, *The Sudbury Town Crier.*

In Florida, Joe Pickett of the golf magazine *The 19th Hole,* down in Bradenton; Mickey Mixon printer/publisher; early editor Sherri Cole, *Sun City Center Observer News*; present editor Brenda Knowles, (who peruses my copy like a hawk!). Peggy Simmons, receptionist at *The Observer News*; Eileen Schipper, proofreader at *The Observer News;* and a very special thanks to Chere Simmons, a writer herself, who scanned, composed, edited, and did everything else that it took to breathe life into "Mulligan." Thanks also to Jon and Celeste at M & M Printing Co., Inc. for their guidance in giving this text a professional wrap-up.

Thanks a million, Chere!

Gratitude is due Helen and Gerry Geddes, Jane Geddes, Mike Sullivan and Karen Latorre of Sullivan and Sperbeck, Walnut Creek, California; Trent Dilfer, quarterback of the Tampa Bay Buccaneers; and Dave Swanson, St. Paul.

Our three sons, Joe, Dan and Steve, are all readers and were brought up being dragged around to: (A) hockey rinks, and (B) bookstores. There is still quite a lot of book exchanging going on in the family. Dan, who is a writer, edited a school paper at the University of Rhode Island, and for two years in a row, captured the prominent Nancy Potter award for fiction at the school. Danny has been a great supporter and assistant for this writing, and in the last two years, we've surely become favorite customers of Ma Bell, between Florida and Connecticut, where he and his wife, Dr. Jane, reside close by her University of Connecticut position. We always end up our discussions with questions such as "What's Robert Parker doing?" or "Have you read John Sanford's latest 'prey' work?" And, of course, we must spend time talking about John Irving, always John Irving, and, his "A Prayer For Owen Meany." Thanks, Dan, very much, for your input.

Here in Sun City Center there is a great group called, The Sun City Center Creative Writers Club. We meet twice a month for several hours at a time. There are about 35 poets and writers in this fraternity and we read to each other, laud and critique one another's work, always in a respectful and friendly atmosphere. There is wonderful talent exhibited throughout these gatherings and we are very proud to sit with these artists, many who have been published over the years.

They are: moderator Della Tyrrell, Chet Buck, Loris Duling, Anita Ewbank, Betty Winn Fuller, Marian Hahn, Herzy Herzberg, Grace Houston, Evelyn Joaquim, Al Jupiter, Cathy Katz, Phil Kats, Bob Larson, Aliza Lavan, Edie Long, Don Looper, Charles Lumm, Louise McArthur, Lee Miles, Erika Nargo, Ed Peattie, Yvonne Ponsor, Edie Pray, George Sagi, Helen Schumacher, Warren Slocum, Sandra Sokol, George Stark, Edna

Watson, George Weber, Skip Winnette, Ann Wood, LeRoy Wright and Robert Andrew Meyer.

Thanks to the following people affiliated with the Mary and Martha House organization: Allen Preston, the late Penny Janes, Dennis Nymark, Marge Ross, Jack Allender, Donna Colbourne, Veronica Mosher, Joe Mullen, Rigmor Rice, Don Rimes, Bill Wheeler, Martin Dodell, Judge Debra Benhke, John Brierley, Pat Clisham, Jean Lampe, Carla Miles, Arlene Oakley, Priscilla Mixon, Thelma Dickman and Marty Logan.

Also thanks to Rick Simone, Craig Janney, Howard Barry and Jack Egan, cartoonists; Mick Elliott and Mike Pennetti of *The Tampa Tribune;* and closing with a warm thanks to Sister Margaret White of my English Composition Oversight Committee.